Managing Emotional Mayhem

The Five Steps for Self-Regulation

by Dr. Becky A. Bailey

Loving Guidance

800.842.2846

P.O. Box 622407, Oviedo FL 32762

ConsciousDiscipline.com

The author of this book may be contacted through Loving Guidance, Inc.

P: 800.842.2846 | F: 407.366.4293 | ConsciousDiscipline.com

ISBN: 978-1-889609-35-5

Cover / Page Design: Brandi Besher

Editor: Julie Ruffo

This book is dedicated to the release of judgment:
The willingness to let go of all preconceptions about what
should be, how it should be and when it should be. Releasing
judgment means learning to be honest with ourselves. It allows
our knowledge to evolve into wisdom, and moves us from
defending to trusting, from separateness to interconnection
and from fear to love.

It is also dedicated to my Mom, Frances Canipe Bailey, and
my Dad, Talmadge Walker Bailey. I thank them for all their
conscious moments and for all their unconscious moments;
both were essential to my growth. They taught me through
compassion and struggle, and taught me to be curious,
love learning, ask questions and reach for my goals.

Contents

Acknowledgements

Many people have participated in the making of this book, some without even knowing how much they contributed. Thank you to my parents, Talmadge and Frances Bailey, for saying, "No." (I gave them countless opportunities, and I mean countless!) Thank you for believing in my ability to handle my upset. I would like to thank my brother, Bud, who relentlessly picked on me, giving me the opportunity to choose between revenge, resignation and resolution. Finally, I am grateful for all the times life did not go my way. I've sure learned some simple lessons the hard way.

As always, an entire community supported this project with the gifts of their time, talent and spirit. First and foremost, I must thank my office family. Every one of them puts their heart and soul into Loving Guidance day after day. Specifically, I offer immense gratitude to Julie Ruffo whose writing and editing make the book enjoyable to read as well as coherent. I often say, "I spray the paper with words and Julie makes it into a masterpiece." A huge hunk of thankfulness goes to Brandi Besher for designing the book from cover to cover. Brandi's creativity is reflected on every page. My appreciation also goes out to Robert Hess for his creative direction and coordinating the efforts of all involved, and to Tracey Tucker for her superb work with the references.

This book is part of a larger project called *The Feeling Buddies Self-Regulation Toolkit* created by Lety Valero and myself. Lety is the principal of Eton School in Mexico City, Mexico. My heartfelt thanks go to Lety, her staff and her students who contributed both inspiration and many of the pictures you see on these pages.

My unending love and appreciation go to Linda Harris, Keith McIntyre and, again, Lety Valero. Each of these dear friends read and reread the manuscript, offering encouragement and writing suggestions. Many others had a hand in making sure this book was done and done well, including the Loving Guidance Associates. They are my sisterhood and the wind beneath my work wings.

Finally, I want to thank you, the reader. Your courage in taking this journey of self-regulation with me contributes to the health of our planet in exponential ways. I am blessed beyond words.

Introduction

Meet Your New BFF:
"Hello, Self-Regulation!"

I can't tell you how many times I've promised myself I'd calm down before speaking when angry, only to find myself yelling at those I love most. I also find myself wanting to lose weight, feeling disappointed with the numbers on the scale and ordering a pizza to feed my unhappiness. I hear the voice of my mother streaming out of my mouth, critically barking commands and questions... even though I know how hurtful this approach felt to me as a child. Sound familiar? I wrote *Managing Emotional Mayhem* for parents and educators because I am ready to do things differently. Since you picked up this book, you're ready, too!

The Unregulated Life

As you can imagine, if we are unable to manage our emotional states in wise ways, we probably aren't very good at helping children manage theirs. "Shut up! I don't want to hear another word out of your mouth." "Go to your room if you can't stop that ridiculous whining. You should know better than this!" "Grow up; nobody said life is fair!" We, as adults, often find ourselves acting out our emotions on children, modeling the exact behaviors we find disturbing. Fueling this fire are thoughts—of who did what, who was wronged and who is guilty—that run wild in our minds like balls in a pinball machine scoring victim and villain points. When our emotional buildup becomes too great to tolerate: Boom! We erupt by verbally or physically attacking others to get temporary relief.

Ultimately, we feel regret for what we've said and done. We pile on the guilt and shame until it obscures our true self from our awareness. We begin to believe we are bad. We justify our actions by creating or reciting life scripts in efforts to protect our worthiness. We base our scripts on how other people made us act a certain way, "I never would have said anything if he hadn't _____." Our scripts support our actions because we believe we were pushed beyond a breaking point, "The child just kept going on and on; what else could I have done!" We create life stories to support all sorts of punishments, "Sometimes you just have to show them who is boss. You know it's for their own good."

The Cycle of Self-Sabotage

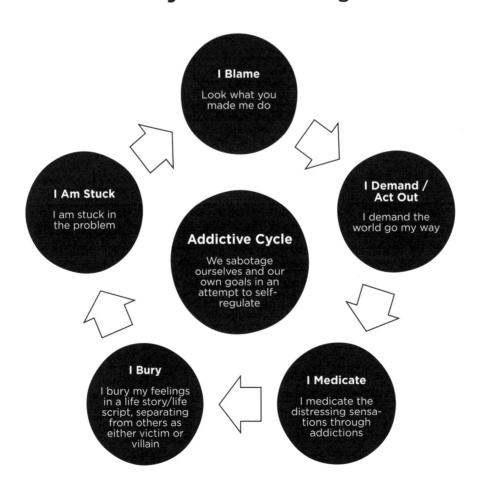

We find ourselves drinking a little too much, eating a little too much, exercising a little too much or working a little too much in efforts to break this cycle of unregulated thoughts and feelings. These unconscious habits become our way of regulating our emotional states. These quirky behaviors and life addictions begin to eat away at our connections with others, ultimately impairing our relationships and goals. We sabotage our own lives in an attempt to regulate our emotions. What a vicious cycle!

The Answer to the Unregulated Life

We are fortunate to live in a time when research and neuroscience provide concrete evidence to support an idea many have long felt to be true: Our relationship with our emotions shapes our brains, our potential for success and the health of all our relationships. We need to make friends with all our emotional states, not just the ones we're comfortable with. We must become buddies with the emotions that derail us.

Every conflict starts with emotional upset. To solve any problem, we must manage the emotional upset first, and then move graciously into a conflict resolution process that produces win-win solutions. Most of us can't make it through the emotional upset to resolve much of anything! We stay stuck in the problem and wedded to our upset, searching outside ourselves for anything to make us feel better. We give our emotional selves away with comments like, "Look what you made me do," "Look how you made your sister feel." We make others responsible for our internal emotional states. "You're driving me nuts." "You're disrupting the learning for all the other students in this classroom." We cling to the idea that others must change for us to feel happy or peaceful, meaning we must control others instead of connect with them. I think we all know how well that has worked for us in the past! As we look at children, we feel compelled to examine and improve our own emotional wellbeing so we can help them develop the healthy emotional compass necessary for lifelong success.

Self-regulation is the foundational component to emotional wellbeing and lifelong success. Self-regulation is the conscious and unconscious ability to regulate our thoughts, feelings and actions in service of a goal. It has been called "self-control" or "impulse control," and these terms are still often used interchangeably. Regulating our thoughts, feelings and actions is different than attempting to control them. We cannot control our emotions any more than we can control the weather. However, we can manage our emotions just as we have learned to bring an umbrella along when it's raining or a heavy coat when it's cold. When we learn to regulate our emotions, we can benefit from the wisdom and moral compass they provide. Without healthy emotional development, we listen to the guidance of the loudest voice in the room instead of the quiet voice within us. For young children, the loudest voice is that of their parents. As they grow up, the voices change to peers, commercialism and ultimately their life partners. The self so vibrant at three years old disappears into self-doubt long before age thirty-three.

Emotions perform many survival functions within the body. The most powerful one is that of integration. Integration is the process of linking differentiated parts together to function as a whole. Our lungs and heart have specialized and differentiated functions, yet we would die if they were not linked together (integrated). Workers in an office have specialized jobs, yet the company fails if they do not communicate well with each other. People of varied ethnicities, who are uniquely differentiated by culture and tradition, enrich communities. Yet, if a community of mixed ethnicities cannot integrate, that community can become weakened by racism and intolerance. The children within a school are unique, but willingness suffers, school climate sours and children are less likely to reach their potential unless they are linked together by a sense of belonging. Integration is essential to the health of our bodies, communities and schools, and ultimately the survival of our planet.

Using the metaphor of a business, integration is a management responsibility. The Director, Principal, Coordinator or CEO has the responsibility to ensure each different department upholds its unique responsibilities and works well with the other departments. Our emotions serve management responsibilities in our brain. They integrate our nervous system in such a way we become a fine-tuned, motivated organism that can be mindful of our thoughts, feelings and actions, see from other people's perspective, solve problems, set and achieve goals, and connect with others. Emotions are the bridge we must cross to get from any problem to its solution. My emotions allow me to become the best Becky I can be and simultaneously contribute to the world in a healthy way. Without access to my emotions, I could easily distort my image of myself to such a degree that I could not contribute to society. In the most extreme situations, I would feel entitled to feed off of or in someway damage the society that sustains me.

How aware are we of our emotions? My best guess is that many of us have the emotional development of a toddler. Do you find this statement shocking or validating? A toddler knows basically two states of being: pleasant and unpleasant. Life is good when I am fed, dry and loved. Life is bad when I am hungry, wet or alone. Ask adults how they are feeling. You generally get two answers: fine and upset. Life is good when it is going my way and upsetting when it is not. Isn't it time we upgraded our emotional awareness?

In this book, you will learn the five steps for self-regulation. These five steps are I Am, I Calm, I Feel, I Choose and I Solve. These steps allow our emotions to perform their integrative duties, and to become the bridge between problem and solution. We must learn to navigate this bridge if we are going to have healthy relationships with our children, life partners and each other. Until we learn a better way and become conscious of habitual reactions, our out-of-control emotions, thoughts and behaviors will become part of another generation that continues to say, "Do what I say, not what I do." At some point, we must decide the buck stops here: I will break the cycle. I will do things differently than was done to me. I will engage in a cycle of success instead of sabotage.

This book is designed to gently step you through a process that will help you shift from sabotage to success. Once we, as adults, have strengthened our skill set, we can begin the process of coaching our children. Check out the goals and the coaching methods you will learn. It's a powerful program, just as we are powerful people.

The Self-Regulation Success Cycle

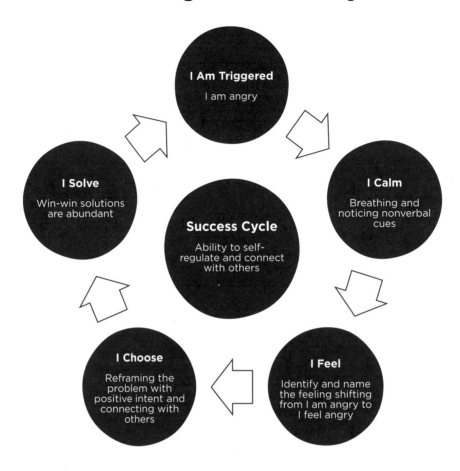

Goals

The overall goal of this book is to achieve better self-regulation for ourselves and our children. See if these specific goals match your most heartfelt desires for personal growth and for the children in your care. Place a check in each box that aligns with your values.

Goals for Adults

In this book, we will learn to (mark the goals *you* want to achieve):

☐ Develop our own self-regulatory skills, providing the opportunity to put a pause between stimulus and response. This pause halts our knee-jerk reactions.

☐ Develop greater awareness of our selves and children, including identifying emotional triggers and accurately naming the feelings involved. This awareness allows emotions to naturally complete their integrative function.

☐ Respond to children's acting out and emotional upset in an attuned way at the moment the event is occurring. This adult response will foster children's development of self-regulation skills.

☐ Coach children to independently use the five-step self-regulation process. As we coach children, we increase their ability to utilize the skills while simultaneously strengthening the same skills within ourselves.

Managing Emotional Mayhem is part of a more comprehensive practice called Conscious Discipline. Conscious Discipline is a complete self-regulation program that integrates social-emotional learning and discipline. It is based on current brain research, and scientifically and practically empowers adults and children to transform conflicts into opportunities to learn critical life skills. If you aren't familiar with Conscious Discipline and wish to learn more, a visit to ConsciousDiscipline.com would be a helpful starting point.

Goals for Our Children

From our learning, we will then be able to help children (mark those you want for your children):

☐ To recognize they have been triggered and begin the self-regulation process.

☐ To begin calming themselves, creating the opportunity to self-regulate.

☐ To name their feeling states and to be able to recognize the feeling states of others. This skill is the foundation for the development of empathy and compassion.

☐ To select and conduct calming and/or engaging strategies in order to shift from an upset state to an optimal learning state.

☐ To learn how to address the upsetting event with greater life skills and solve their problem.

☐ To develop social awareness, responsible decision-making and communication skills aimed at fostering healthy relationships and goal achievement. As children repeat the five-step process again and again, their moral compass directs them in healthy ways to communicate, make decisions and problem-solve.

Coaching Methods

Coaching during teachable moments. In the world of young children, emotional upset is triggered every day. Limits are set, rules are enforced and the world does not always go their way. Instead of dismissing children's upset, sending children to time out, giving rewards or removing privileges, we can respond to these moments in a way that transforms conflict into cooperation. In Conscious Discipline we call these "teachable moments" instead of "discipline disruptions." Teachable moments require us to coach children to change their internal emotional states first. Then we teach a new behavioral skill. When we focus on internal states first and behaviors second, we create an opportunity to use conflict as a tool for learning social and life skills. Adults are empowered to seize these discipline disruptions as teachable moments in order to provide children with new social-emotional and self-regulatory skills.

I never knew how powerful my response to my kids' upset could possibly be. I truly thought my job was to get them to behave properly. If I got them in bed on time, out the door on time, to say please and thank you, and finish their homework, I'd have this parenting gig down. One day my oldest started running his mouth (as usual) and instead of giving him a stern look and reminding him how rude he was being, I said, "You seem angry. You were hoping you could spend more time with your friends this afternoon." His whole being changed! I changed, he changed and since then our relationship has changed. I love my new BFF – self-regulation. If I had not calmed down and seen past his mouth (one he learned mostly from me, I admit), I would have never been able to help him.

Wishing you well,
Toni, mother of 3 boys

Coaching in the Safe Place. The Safe Place is one of the core social-emotional learning structures in the Conscious Discipline philosophy. It is an area in the home or classroom where children can practice using self-regulatory skills. If you are not familiar with the Safe Place, I invite you to explore Shubert's Classroom at Conscious Discipline.com to see images and video of this essential structure. We will also learn much about the Safe Place in Chapter 5.

Going to the Safe Place to practice self-regulatory techniques when emotions are triggered is crucial for success. This is because the brain is state-dependent. The brain can only rewire itself for behavioral changes through repetitive actions conducted while experiencing a given state. A child can sing about anger, role-play anger management skills and identify angry faces, yet may be unable to regulate her own angry feelings and actions. This is because she can only learn to regulate her anger when an angry brain-body state is activated. In the Safe Place, children experience intense emotions and handle them in such a way that their brains actually become wired with new behaviors based on self-regulation strategies.

Unifying Parents and Educators

Parents and educators have spent generations speaking different languages when it comes to discipline. Educators have demanded parents make their children behave at school, while parents have repeatedly said, "We don't have this problem at home." At our best, we've gained a bit of insight from each other in 15-minute parent-teacher meetings and the occasional school event. At our worst, we've pointed fingers of fault at each other's perceived deficiencies. It is long overdue for us all to get on the same page. I believe that integrating home and school is an essential step in societal growth. Self-regulation and impulse control do not emerge spontaneously. They are skills, learned not only through families and cultures, but also through schools and teachers (Nagin & Tremblay, 1999). I wrote this book in hopes of literally bringing parents and educators together on the same page. Page by page, we can improve our own self-regulation skill set and learn ways to help children develop healthy skills for themselves. May we take the fingers we point at each other and instead link them together in a commitment to become the best adults we can!

My intent is to unite homes and schools in a common goal of social-emotional success; however, I recognize that each group has unique concerns and logistics. For this reason, I have developed two specialized self-regulation toolkits, one for parents and one for educators. These toolkits are an extension of this book, and are based on the Feeling Buddies. The Feeling Buddies are eight simple gingerbread dolls with precise emotions expressed on their faces: angry, sad, scared, happy, frustrated, disappointed, anxious and calm. The adult teaches children how to help their Buddies self-regulate. In doing this, both adult and child practice and teach the same process to themselves. The Buddies are occasionally mentioned in this book, and are a valuable part of the self-regulation process. My hope is that this book will inspire you to continue your journey with self-regulation. The *Feeling Buddies Self-Regulation Toolkit for Educators* and the *Feeling Buddies Self-Regulation Toolkit for Parents* provide the means to that end.

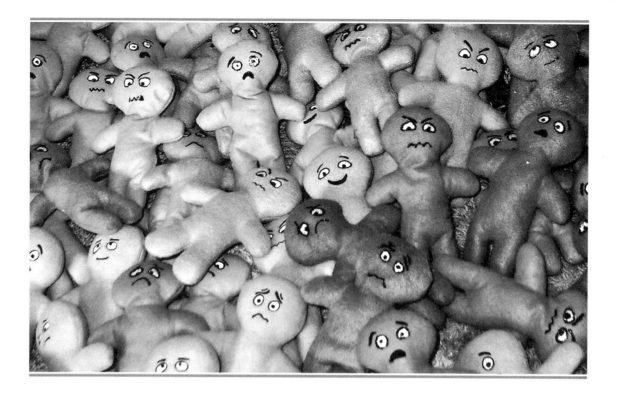

Whether you are an educator or parent or both, one thing I know for sure is that feelings can sometimes be overwhelming for us all.

Book Overview

There are no accidents. You have purchased this book at precisely the right time and will get from it exactly what you need. Whether you choose to delve deeper by adding a *Self-Regulation Toolkit* to your journey is a personal decision. This book alone will set a solid course, and may be all you need to right your ship.

This book contains five chapters. Chapter 1 provides foundational information about self-regulation. Many of you may not be overly familiar with this term. You probably have guessed it is related to impulse control, self-control and emotional control, but is there more to it? In Chapter 1, I will reveal and explore the many facets of self-regulation. Chapter 2 will ask you to clean out your proverbial closet by reflecting on your relationship with your emotions and how you were disciplined as a child. Chapter 3 begins to fill your closet with a new understanding of the messages of feelings. Chapter 4 guides you through the five-step self-regulation process so you can begin to practice and model what you ultimately expect from children. Chapter 5 provides you with the information and dialogues to coach children through the five-step self-regulation process.

I started this introduction by sharing ways my own thoughts, feelings and actions often sabotage what I most desire. In the pages since, we've dipped our toes in a pool of new knowledge and self-reflection. Take a moment to ask yourself, "Do my thoughts, feelings and actions support my most valued goals or sabotage them? Am I on the success cycle or the sabotage cycle?" I have already committed myself to do things differently. Are you ready to join me? If so, our journey starts now. Enjoy the ride!

Commitment: I commit to managing my inner mayhem. I am willing to do things differently, accept what is and move forward toward solutions. I will no longer blame others for my upset or demand life go my way. I understand this practice will strengthen all my relationships, including my relationship with myself. It reveals to me my basic worth, which is hidden beneath guilt that I am ready to release.

Signed: *Becky A. Bailey*　　　　Date: Starting right now!

I willingly commit to join Becky on this essential journey.

Signed: _____　　Date: _____

Chapter

Self-Regulation:
The Bedrock of Emotional Wellbeing and Healthy Relationships

We are all born with a deep genetic need to be in relationships with others. Our survival depends on this connection. Maybe this is why we yearn for that perfect mate, deep friendships and unconditional acceptance. Unfortunately, we find ourselves drowning in perpetual conflict more often than we feel dipped in loving harmony. In order to form successful relationships with others, we must first establish a stable emotional foundation within ourselves. This stable foundation is called "emotional wellbeing" and is dependent on the skill of self-regulation. Self-regulation and emotional wellbeing are the glue that holds us together. It allows us to develop empathy so we can see the world through the eyes of others. It fosters a sense of compassion where we seek to relieve the suffering of others. Without the ability to regulate our thoughts, feelings and actions, being close to others all too often brings us pain instead of a joyful bond, and our world of unity splits rapidly into separate entities fighting with each other.

Almost everyone I know has said the following words: "When I grow up, I will never _____ my children." Or "When I grow up, I will never treat another human being like that." Yet, it didn't take us long to break these promises to

ourselves. In its simplest form, this book helps us repair our fractured foundations and helps children develop strong foundations for emotional wellbeing
by learning the five steps to self-regulation.

> Doing it differently than was done to us requires we become consciously
> aware of our emotions, willing to learn how to regulate their intensity
> and skillful in communicating them to others. Without the above skills,
> emotions can become weapons instead of tools.

Emotional Wellbeing

"Emotional wellbeing" is an umbrella term for emotional intelligence (EQ) and
social emotional learning (SEL). It broadly describes an internal state of emotional health. I've chosen to use the term emotional wellbeing throughout this
book because of the wealth of definitions existing regarding the terms EQ and
SEL, and the significant overlap in research, application and understanding of
each term.

> Emotional intelligence and social-emotional learning deal with fostering
> social-emotional development. Emotional intelligence, as introduced by
> Daniel Goleman (1995, 1998), is a form of aptitude relating to our emo-
> tional lives. It includes such skills as the ability to recognize and manage
> emotions, motivation, impulse restraint and effective handling of rela-
> tionships. The Collaborative for Academic, Social and Emotional Learn-
> ing (CASEL), an organization dedicated to advancing the science of
> social-emotional learning, has identified five core social emotional com-
> petencies: self-awareness, self-management, social awareness, relation-
> ship skills and responsible decision-making.

Emotional wellbeing equals mental, physical, social and cognitive health. Significant amounts of research now exists in regard to our emotions, their de-

velopment, and their impact on life and school success. The core features of emotional wellbeing include the ability to:

- Identify and understand one's own feelings.
- Accurately read and comprehend emotional states in others.
- Manage the expression of strong emotions in a constructive manner.
- Regulate one's own behavior.
- Develop empathy for others.
- Establish and sustain relationships.
  (National Scientific Counsel on the Developing Child, 2005)

Pause for a moment to reflect on your own emotional wellbeing. Can you identify what you are feeling at the time you are feeling it? If you are like me, it could take hours, weeks and sometimes years to figure out the true feeling in a given situation. At the Loving Guidance office, I would often become angry and express that anger in inappropriate ways. Months later, I would reflect on those moments only to discover that behind my anger I was feeling fearful and overwhelmed. Years later, I see the situation with different eyes. I was afraid we would fail and equally afraid we would succeed. Either way, I felt the responsibility for Loving Guidance was mine and mine alone. This erroneous perception created a great deal of stress within me. Now I know our office team and divine forces are in this together. The burden of success or failure is not on my shoulders; it's not even part of my job description! My job is to be the best me possible, and all else will fall into place.

Self-Regulation

Self-regulation is the ability to regulate our thoughts, feelings and actions. It is at the core of emotional wellbeing for academic and life success. It is the essential skill that allows us to put a pause between impulse and action (Vohs & Baumeister, 2004). Imagine what life would be like if we acted on every thought we had, every impulse generated and all the emotional distress we felt. I could eat two gallons of ice cream, run over at least one slow person crossing the street and create a

> Research identifies self-regulation as the foundation for our performance in all domains from reading to getting along with others.
> - Lyon & Krasnegor, 1996

children's television series — all before noon!

Our capacity for conscious and voluntary self-regulation gives us control over primitive instincts and survival reactions. It allows choice, decision-making and planning. Regulating our impulses is essential for following the rules, achieving goals, and maintaining personal commitments and relationships. Our ability to live peacefully with freedom and responsibility depends on it (Bronson, 2000).

As mentioned in the introduction, this book is an outgrowth of my program Conscious Discipline. The Conscious Discipline program's brain model is based on brain states and their relationship to behavior. In Conscious Discipline, we talk about lower, survival-based brain states and higher, integrated states (Bailey, 2011). Brain research shows that self-regulation is a higher-order skill linked to the maturation of the prefrontal lobe (commonly referred to as the CEO of the brain). The prefrontal lobes house the executive skills. These skills allow us to set and achieve goals, focus our attention despite distractions, get along with others, offer empathy and problem solve. Without self-regulation, none of these skills can fully mature or come online. School success, life success and relationship success are all at risk without this basic skill.

The ability to control our impulses in order to stop doing something (especially if we want to continue doing it) and to start doing something that is needed or healthy (especially if we don't want to do it) is a tough skill to master but one that is essential. We can help children, starting in early childhood, to make significant progress toward emotional wellbeing and self–regulation by providing attuned, responsive guidance. One of the goals of the early childhood years is to develop the ability for the higher brain centers in the prefrontal lobe to override impulses from the lower centers of the brain. In Conscious Discipline (Bailey, 2000; 2011), I call this "moving from unconsciously reacting to consciously responding to life events." Regulation of internal states is essential in this process.

Basically there are two response styles to children's display of negative emotions. They are "emotion coaching," which you will learn in this book, and "emotion dismissive," which most of us learned through our family culture. Emotion coaching considers children's expression of emotion as an opportunity to validate their inner world and teach them about emotions, expression and coping. Emotion coaching says, "Emotions have value." Parenting in this style increases children's capacity to regulate emotions, and develop self-esteem, empathy and compassion for others. The emotion dismissing style views emotions as dangerous, and focuses on avoiding or minimizing them. Emotion dismissing parenting is a risk factor for poor emotional regulation, behavioral problems and lack of empathy in children (Gottman et al, 1996; Kanat-Maymom & Assor, 2010; Lunkenheimer, Shields & Cortina, 2007). We will explore these styles in detail in Chapter 2. For now, it is important to know what research and common sense tell us.

- There is a growing wave of concern that young children are not entering school with the self-regulatory skills that they need (Raver & Knitzer, 2002). *Have you noticed more out-of-control children with more difficult behavior problems?*

- Parents who are controlling have children who are angrier and less empathetic (Strayer & Roberts, 2004). *Does a family who fits this dynamic come to mind?*

- In some early childhood centers, there were six or more instances of serious aggressive behavior a day (Kupersmidt, Bryant, & Willoughby, 2000; Willoughby, Kupersmidt, & Bryant, 2001). *What would the research show in your school? Has your child been involved in an aggressive incident or witnessed this aggression?*

- When preschool teachers fail to handle social-emotional problems well, they perpetuate unregulated behaviors in their young pupils and pass the problem up through the ages where change is much more difficult (Arnold, McWilliams, & Arnold, 1998). *Do you think this has changed significantly since 1998?*

- Controlling parents who suppress or dismiss their children's feelings have children who grow up with two deficits in emotional development: 1) Poor recognition of emotions in themselves and others. 2) Less empathetic support for their partner especially when that partner is experiencing difficulties (Roth et. al, 2009). *Think about your circle of adult friends and colleagues. Does it seem like any of them might have experienced or are perpetuating this type of upbringing?*

- Teachers report they feel overwhelmed and do not know what to do to support their young students. In an increasing number of cases, children with behavioral problems are simply being expelled from classrooms (Gilliam, 2005, Raver & Knitzer, 2002). *Are you hopeful for the future or too exhausted to truly advocate on behalf of children and families?*

- Teacher burnout from dealing with out-of-control children is skyrocketing (Hastings, 2003). *If you are a teacher, how have you changed since you entered the profession? If you are a parent, how has school changed since you were young?*

The grave outcomes from a lack of self-regulation make it clear just how important it is for us to address emotional wellbeing. As adults, we must begin by confronting our own self-regulatory and emotional wellbeing issues. We must comprehend on a deeper level that the way we interact with children will foster or inhibit their ability to develop optimal self-regulation. This requires us to examine our relationship with our emotions and be willing to upgrade our emotional intelligence for the betterment of our children and our collective future. This book will help both you and your children. If we do not address self-regulation effectively and guide our children differently, we can expect devastating consequences. The following research offers us a glimpse of a future without self-regulation:

- If early childhood-aged children do not practice self-regulation enough, the related brain areas will not fully develop and the end result may be adults who still act like they are in their "terrible twos." (Boyd, Barnett, Bodrova, Leong, & Gomby, 2005). *When was the last time you threw a fit?*

- Two decades of research found that self-regulation, not IQ scores or entry-level reading and math skills, is directly related to successful academic performance (Bronson & Merryman, 2009). *Have you noticed that the children with behavioral problems also have academic struggles?*

- We are fundamentally egocentric and have difficulty getting beyond our own perspective. Without self-regulation we are unable to move beyond our innate default button of projecting self-traits onto others (Decety &

Hodges, 2006). *Have you noticed what you judge in others is what you fear about yourself?*

- Children lacking emotional self-regulation are at higher risk for disciplinary problems and are less likely to make a successful transition from preschool to kindergarten (Huffman, Mehlinger, & Kerivan, 2001). *If you are a teacher, how often have you thought, "If he could just stay with me another year..."? How often as a parent have you questioned whether your child is ready for preschool, kindergarten or whatever that next step is?*

> Emotional self-regulation seems to play a part in child resiliency and later adjustments to life's challenges.
>
> - Eisenberg et. al., 2004

- Children who do not learn self-regulation in preschool can turn into bullies with aggressive habits of interaction that are difficult to break in later years (Nagin & Tremblay, 1999; Shonkoff & Phillips 2000). *Being deeply honest, how many children have you believed could grow up to land in jail?*

- Motivation is directly linked to self-regulation. We are innately and intrinsically motivated to self-regulate. We are wired to be helpful, of service and cooperative. We must learn how to develop this genetic system instead of replace it with external controls (Bailey, 2011). ***Have you noticed a four-year-old who is excited about learning transform into an eight-year-old who says, "What do I get if I am good?"***

The Relationship Between Discipline and Self-Regulation

Most of us were raised in a culture that believed "discipline equals punishment." Parents thought discipline was something they did to children to make them behave properly, not something to develop within them. Teachers thought discipline had little to do with relationships; it was a system provided, purchased or adopted to maintain order. The goal was to teach children to be good boys and girls; to be respectful. "Respectful" was a code word for "compliant". Discipline was a one-way street, from adult to child. We had no idea discipline had anything to do with relationships, current or future. We did not know that how we addressed conflict with or between children would either foster or inhibit their ability to self-regulate for the rest of their lives.

Most of us are familiar with external, judgment-based models for discipline and guidance. If we judge a child to be good, she receives some kind of reward. If we judge a child to be bad, we take away a toy, remove a privilege or she receives something undesirable like a referral to the principal's office or a spanking. This external system is a simple stimulus-response paradigm: We judge the child as good or bad, and we provide the matching external consequence. There is no pause in this traditional reward and punishment system. It is not a stimulus-pause-response system of self-guidance and higher order thinking. It does not teach self-regulation or self-control. It teaches other-control and outer-regulation.

Children raised in a household based on rewards and punishments have a difficult time making a shift from relying on others for guidance to becoming proficient at listening to their own wisdom. Their "discipline" comes from outside forces, not from within themselves. Throughout life, they continue to seek things, situations and other people as their moral compass. As children, they listen to the judgments of adults to determine if they are good or bad human beings. As teenagers, they listen to friends to guide their personal choices. In relationships, they depend on the mood of their partner to guide their happiness. Unless they consciously change, they will rely on external forces to govern themselves rather than trust their own internal guidance.

Children react on an emotional level (from the lower centers of their brain) long before they can verbalize their experience or discern ways to cope with life (Greenberg & Snell, 1997). Discipline in early childhood requires us to help children advance from lower brain centers of emotional reactions to higher brain centers that allow them to respond to the situational demands of that moment. In the lower brain regions, a child's arousal level plus her desires equals behavior. "I want it, I take it. If I don't get it, I scream, bite, grab or hit." The prefrontal lobes of the higher centers of the brain allow children to override these basic impulses and replace them with self-regulatory skills such as frustration tolerance, emotional management and problem-solving skills. For example: "I want it. I ask for a turn. If I don't get it, I manage the disappointment. I'm then able to wait or find something else to do."

Conscious Discipline prepares us to build the foundations of classrooms and homes by using safety, connection and problem-solving rather than rewards and punishments. In this way, we are able to teach children how to self-regulate by developing the pause between a stimulus and a response. The pause in Conscious Discipline is the ability to self-regulate, to consciously identify and manage our inner states so we can be the person we believe ourselves to be. When we feel angry, we are not locked into hitting or name-calling. With Conscious Discipline we learn to say, "I don't like it when you push me. Please walk around me." We learn to use the energy of anger to motivate us to shift our reactions into healthy responses, sustaining our relationships. This book harnesses the power of Conscious Discipline to help adults create this self-regulatory pause for themselves and the children in their care.

Safety

Connection

Problem-Solving

Children need adults to guide them. This guidance is embedded in the relationship the child has with each adult. Parents provide children with their primary bond. Educators often provide secondary bonds, so educators must acknowledge the power and purpose of establishing healthy relationships with all children in their care. It is incumbent upon teachers to fulfill the job of teaching self-regulation as well as the ABCs.

The following chart shows the difference in the belief structure between traditional discipline of rewards and punishments and Conscious Discipline.

Traditional Discipline	Conscious Discipline
It is possible to control others through environmental manipulations.	Controlling and changing ourselves is possible and has a profound impact on others.
Rules govern behavior.	Connectedness governs behavior.
Conflict is a disruption to the learning process.	Conflict is an opportunity to teach.

Most traditional discipline models explicitly or implicitly teach children one of the following:

1. **They are responsible for the feelings of others.** *"Look how you made your brother feel." "You are making this family dinner miserable." "You're driving me crazy." "You are preventing all the other*

children from learning." We unconsciously place children in charge of the emotional states of adults and other children, leaving them irresponsible for their own behaviors.

2. **They are told what they should be feeling.** *"You should be ashamed of yourself for acting like that." "You should feel bad." "Look what you have done! Are you happy now?"* Telling children what to feel robs them of experiencing their own internal guidance.

3. **Feelings are dangerous; they can and will hurt you.** *"You don't want me upset." "If I have to get involved, you both will be in serious trouble." "Your father is furious, wait until he gets home." "You want to cry? I'll give you something to cry about!" "Oh honey, it's not that bad, let's go get some ice cream." "Don't you worry, I'll take care of everything. You aren't in any trouble." "I'll go to your school and talk to your teacher. Everyone forgets his homework now and again."* If you were taught your feelings are dangerous, wouldn't you want to avoid them?

These beliefs, unconsciously handed down from generation to generation, separate the child from an awareness of his own internal emotional states and his inherent wisdom. These beliefs erode his ability to trust himself and, in turn, to trust others. They teach him that empathy isn't valuable, getting your way equals happiness and peace of mind, and controlling others equals self-regulation. Two deeply troubling mental health issues arise from this approach. First, it impedes creating and sustaining healthy relationships with significant others. Secondly, it embeds the notion that something outside of ourselves will bring us happiness and peace. Most of us seem to have lived most of our lives thinking money, things or other people are a source of happiness, only to discover that these things are fleeting and unreliable at best. Conscious Discipline and the five steps to self-regulation presented in this book help us to replace these unhealthy emotional patterns.

When we are finally willing to look within, we discover happiness is a choice, not an event. We find we can choose to remain peaceful during the most difficult moments. After all of our searching for the perfect home, children, partners, jobs and bodies, it seems we have come to know that happiness is inherently ours. As we discover this for our adult selves, we also feel a strong desire to help children experience a different kind of discipline than we experienced. We can offer attuned responses to children's inner states as part of the discipline process. As we experience the peace and joy of reclaiming our own emotional guidance, we can empower children to do the same. We can bring peace to any problem. This is the power of Conscious Discipline and the five steps to self-regulation.

Conscious Discipline and Self-Regulation

Two cornerstone beliefs in Conscious Discipline provide the basis for the five steps to self-regulation that allow us to discipline differently than we were disciplined.

1. **What you offer to others, you strengthen within yourself.** If you offer calmness in a difficult situation, you strengthen your ability to be of service. If you offer criticism to others, you will ultimately feel inadequate about yourself. As you teach children to manage their emotional states, you become more adept at managing your own.

2. **Whoever you believe to be in charge of your feelings, you have placed in charge of you.** If traffic *makes* you angry then traffic is in charge of you. If children *make* you frustrated, then you have placed

the children in charge. If your significant other *makes* you happy, then you have placed him or her in charge. When you make traffic, children and partners responsible for your internal feeling states, they have the power and the responsibility to *make* things better or worse for you. You are powerless to change and dependent on others for happiness and peace of mind. You are a victim to life. Instead, we can choose to use self-regulation to be in charge of our feelings, reclaim our personal power and be responsible for ourselves.

What you offer to others you strengthen within yourself. If we offer *condemnation* to others, we feel *not good enough* ourselves. If we offer *well wishes* to others, we feel *peaceful* inside. The process goes like this: As I write these words to teach you, I get better at the self-regulation process with myself. When you coach and teach children the process, you strengthen your own self-regulation skills. As the children teach and coach their Feeling Buddies (more about this in Chapter 5), they grow in their social and emotional competence. It is a powerful program where everybody wins. Our collective emotional wellbeing prospers as each of us make this committed effort. The best way to learn anything is to teach it to others. It is reminiscent of the story of the dog who chased the cat, the cat who ate the rat and the rat who ate the cheese, except in this case we help the children, they help their Feeling Buddies and we all enjoy wellbeing. Whether or not you purchase a *Feeling Buddies Self-Regulation Toolkit* is not important. What's important is that we learn about and embrace the five steps to self-regulation so we each may become the person we truly know ourselves to be.

Whoever you believe to be in charge of your feelings, you have placed in charge of you. When we attempt to make others responsible for our feelings, we also give them the responsibility and power to make us feel better. In essence, my upset is your fault and you must change for me to have internal peace and happiness. In workshops, I use a beach ball to demonstrate this point. I use a large black marker and print the words "Feelings," "Power" and "Responsibility" on the ball. The beach ball represents the idea that whoever is in charge of the *feelings* also has the *power* and *responsibility* to make changes. We then role-play different scenarios, and participants forcefully throw or gently hand the beach ball back and forth to show emotional ownership (you can see an example of this on the *Feeling Buddies DVD*). The scene below describes the tossing of the ball (who owns your feelings) between Joshua and his teacher, Ms. Glenda. Watch how Joshua and his teacher each attempt to make the other responsible for the upset.

Ms. Glenda: "Joshua, it's time to clean up. Pick up all the blocks and put them on the shelves." (Ms. Glenda is in charge of her inner state. She keeps the ball representing power, feeling and responsibility, and Joshua is in charge of his.)

Joshua ignores the teacher and continues to build. (Ms. Glenda is still in charge of her inner state, still holding the ball, and Joshua is in charge of his.)

However, Ms. Glenda is feeling tired today and is in no mood to deal with Joshua.

Ms. Glenda: "Joshua, I do *not* have time for this today. Pick up the blocks this instant! Don't make this hard." (Ms. Glenda forcefully throws the ball to Joshua. Her nonverbal and verbal message is *you are making me upset*.)

Joshua: "Shut up and leave me alone." (Joshua throws the ball back at Ms. Glenda with this attacking language. His message is *I will not be in charge of your feelings, you are!*)

Ms. Glenda: "Don't you talk to me like that. It is disrespectful. I won't have it! Go to time out this minute. Don't make me have to walk over there." (Ms. Glenda, more intensely upset, forcefully throws the ball back to Joshua. Her message is *you better start making me feel better or you will be in worse trouble than before*.)

> Joshua kicks down all the blocks in a two-foot radius around him, then pushes other toys off a shelf and attempts to hit Ms. Glenda. (Joshua proclaims his resistance to be in charge of Ms. Glenda's upset state. His message is *I will not be responsible for your upset.*)

Do you see how Ms. Glenda repeatedly gave her power away to Joshua, demanding he change so she could find peace of mind? Joshua resisted, leaving both of them with a feeling of powerlessness. From that powerless state, attack and blame followed, and the problem escalated.

Projecting our inability to identify, own and name our feelings onto those around us results in a very dangerous logic: *If you make me angry, you are at fault and you must change for me to feel better. If you make me angry then I must control you in order to regulate me.* Alternately, learning to identify, own and name our own feelings results in the following healthy logic: *If I feel angry, I can choose to manage my own feelings and use them to motivate me to change. I can regulate myself and communicate with you.* We each choose whether to create resentment through blame or to build love through sharing.

Children are born with an internal emotional guidance system that is immature, at best. Since adults put limits on children's desires and actions, children believe their internal emotional states are caused by the actions of adults. Adults make them mad, sad, scared or happy. However, the adult's job is to slowly hand over this responsibility to the child. As children grow, the adult must set limits on behaviors while simultaneously teaching children that they are in charge of their own feelings and teaching them how to regulate their inner world. The goal of discipline is for adults to empower children to manage themselves. This can only occur if they learn to be aware of their emotions, regulate them and listen to their internal wisdom to guide them to the next best step in life.

Instead of attempting to make children feel bad for the distress they have triggered within us or trying to save them from the distress they feel from making poor choices, we can do it differently. Telling children what to feel or saving them from what they are feeling misses the mark. Going back to the beach ball analogy, we still end up holding their beach ball; we are still responsible for regulating their behavior and they are responsible for regulating ours. Instead, look at what is possible if we learn to feel, manage and regulate our own internal states:

Ms. Glenda: "Joshua, it is time to clean up. Pick up all the blocks and put them on the shelves." (Ms. Glenda is in charge of her inner state, holding the ball, and Joshua is in charge of his.)

Joshua ignores the teacher and continues to build. (No tossing. Ms. Glenda is in charge of her inner state and Joshua is in charge of his.)

Ms. Glenda is feeling tired today and is in no mood to deal with Joshua. She consciously recognizes this frustration brewing within. She takes a deep calming breath and says to herself, *I'm safe, keep breathing. I can handle this.* Once she is calm, she walks over to Joshua, waits for him to make eye contact and helps him shift his focus from playing to cleaning up.

Ms. Glenda: "Joshua, there you are. It is time to clean up. You have a choice. You can clean up the cars first or the blocks you used for roads. Which is better for you?" (Ms. Glenda is in charge of her inner state and gives the ball to Joshua with the opportunity for him to take charge of his inner state through choices.)

Joshua: "Shut up and leave me alone." (Joshua throws the ball at Ms. Glenda with his attacking language. The message is *I am angry and it is your fault.*)

Ms. Glenda: "You seem angry. You were hoping you could play longer and finish your roads. It is hard to stop and clean up. You can handle this, Joshua. Breathe with me." Ms. Glenda takes a slow deep breath to help Joshua calm down enough to manage his anger. (Ms. Glenda gently hands Joshua the ball, empowering him to be responsible for his next choice.)

Joshua: "I wanted to keep building." (Joshua is empowered to communicate his desires. He is able to hold his beach ball.)

Ms. Glenda: "You worked hard to create your roads. It's hard to stop. You can do it. You have a choice. You can start with your cars or the roads. Which would help you get started?"

Joshua: "The cars."

Ms. Glenda: "There you go. That's it. You are doing it. Good for you."

The power of self-regulation versus other-control is evident. Ms. Glenda was able to manage her frustration enough to help Joshua manage his anger and disappointment. We have a choice, we can beat children up with our emotions or we can coach them in how to manage theirs.

Maybe you have seen online videos of young children giggling hysterically as an adult tears up pieces of paper or something similar. Small children seem to delight in most everything! They naturally do something we forget to do. They bring their delight with them instead of demanding outside events provide it.

The Relationship Between Self-Regulation and Emotions

Most folks just think, "If I can get control of my emotions, all will be well." Self-regulation is not about emotional control or a lack of it. It is an integrative process that comes about by allowing our unconscious emotions to become conscious feelings. The flow of energy from the lower centers to the higher centers of the brain integrates the mind, body and brain to allow us to become aware of the helpful signals our emotions provide. As a result, we take the wisest action possible.

We are social beings with social brains. Emotions alert us to the action that is needed to survive and sustain relationships. A child's anxiety when his mother leaves the room primes the mother and child to stay close, promoting the child's survival. Anger (often expressed through aggression, tantrums and defiance) is a psychological signal that directs us to change our behavior, much like the physiological signals of thirst, hunger and tiredness direct us to drink, eat and sleep. Ignoring our children's emotional states risks social emotional malnourishment, much like ignoring their hunger risks physical malnourishment.

According to Bruce Perry (2001), healthy self-regulation is related to the capacity to tolerate the sensations of distress that accompany an unmet need. When an infant feels hunger, she also feels discomfort and distress. She communicates this distress to others by crying. Hopefully, an attuned adult will read her signals and respond by feeding her to reduce the discomfort and distress. After thousands of such interactions, the infant learns that the distress (emotional upset) is tolerable, is manageable and will pass.

Attuned adult responses are needed for a child's self-regulatory system to mature. Let's use anxiety as an example. An attuned adult knows "anxious" is a call for comfort and possibly additional information (see Chapter 3). The attuned Mom dropping her child off at Ms. Becky's preschool might say, "It's scary when I leave. Ms. Becky will keep you safe. I will return after naptime. Breathe with me, baby. You are safe." Sadly, we are more likely to hear, "You're okay. Go with Ms. Becky. You know I always come back. Now give Mommy a kiss." Or, "If you go with Ms. Becky and be good, we'll stop at McDonald's after

I pick you up." Without attunement, the flow of energy from the lower centers to the higher centers of the brain is blocked and the child is stuck in a state of distress. After thousands of such interactions, the child learns that distress (emotional upset) is not tolerable, is best managed through approval or food, and will not pass without appeasing others.

The attuned, responsive adult helps the child create a momentary pause between the impulse (anxiety) and the action (going into preschool). The process is the same for all emotional states. If a child signals sadness, anger or embarrassment, an attuned adult can pick up on this communication and coach the child through her discomfort to an integrated state. The child will learn that emotions are a bridge between problem and solution, reducing the likelihood of a reactive (e.g. tantrum) or impulsive (e.g. hitting, name-calling) response. As the attuned adult continues this coaching process over time, the child matures with the ability to self-regulate: He is able to put a pause between a feeling and an action, knowing distress is temporary and will pass at some point. His feelings are manageable and tolerable. This pause allows him to access his own wisdom or allows him to be willing to be coached to think, plan and come up with an appropriate response as demonstrated by Ms. Glenda and Joshua in the second example.

Feelings are the bridge between problems and solutions.

Our Emotional Guidance System (EGS)

Historically, the worthiness of emotions has been questioned. Eastern cultures once believed an excess of emotions caused damage to the life force, while the western world viewed emotions as immoral and inferior to reason. Now, emotions often take center stage. The hard sciences and common sense have joined in the recognition that emotions are not only good for us, they are essential for cognition, brain development, physical health and happiness. Emotions provide us with an internal guidance system.

Many people have access to a Global Positioning System, or GPS, for navigation. These navigational systems provide us with guidance while on the roads. They tell us how to reach our goals, giving us commands such as, "Turn left in half of a mile." If we follow a GPS, there is a very good chance we will arrive at our destination. If we get off track, it recalculates a new path or re-routes us back to the original course. We also have an emotional system that serves a similar purpose. It is called the "Emotional Guidance System" or EGS.

Our EGS is not an add-on feature or device, it is an intrinsic system of emotions. It focuses our attention, gives us important information about a given situation, motivates us to communicate with others and allows us to adapt to varying circumstances. We all have access to our EGS. Some of us will develop it into a complex, regulated system that guides us towards wisdom. Others will let it linger as a survival-level, reactionary system. Accordingly, it can bring us closer to each other with intense love or separate us with painful experiences.

Parenting and teaching children in a way that fosters the healthy maturation of their EGS requires our willingness to consciously put the child in touch with her EGS instead of distracting, distancing or overlaying it with our insecurities. When we develop a healthy EGS, we are able to turn inward, to take responsibility for our actions and learn from our mistakes. When we let it atrophy, we seek external sources of comfort and validation, spiral into addiction, and seek to distract ourselves from difficult emotions as we look outside of ourselves for guidance. The state of our EGS will dictate the type of EGS we foster within the children in our care. We simply cannot teach or model healthy emotional guidance for children if we don't possess it ourselves.

Emotions are, in essence, a vehicle of change (Damasio, 1999). Our EGS brings our attention to the fact that something has changed—for good or for bad—and signals us to deal with it. Emotions are to the psychological body as pain is to the physical body. Physical pain is a signal that says, "Hey you! Over here!" It calls you to action, perhaps to get off your feet for a while, watch what you eat or see the doctor. Physical pain does not get your attention in hopes you will deny it, suffer with it, use it as an excuse for not living fully or push through it. It calls you to be curious, to notice what makes it worse or better and to be mindfully alert to the needed action. Pain wants you to return your body to harmony so that all of the systems are in healthy relationship with one another. *Emotional discomfort has the exact same purpose.* It draws our attention to something, allowing us to discover the action needed to sustain healthy relationships with each other and make wise decisions.

Each emotion contains an automatic action tendency that's evolutionarily designed to give us the resources to deal with whatever triggered it. Our EGS guides us from the problem to the action that is the wisest solution. When used optimally, our EGS serves a transformative, integrated function that helps us regulate our emotions, allows us to integrate higher and lower centers of our brain, and leads us to our own unique wisdom about situations and events.

> **Pain wants you to return your body to harmony so that all of the systems are in healthy relationship with one another.**

Embracing Our Emotions

Our attitude toward our emotions is crucial. I often hear adults say, "Oh, I just can't let myself be angry. I would be angry for twenty years!" These adults are simply saying, "I didn't grow up with an attuned adult to help me know my anger is manageable and my sense of distress would, indeed, pass." If we see emotions as dangerous or frightening, then we can only manage our emotions (and the emotions of others) by responding with social pressure, punishment, avoidance and/or fear tactics. Alternatively, if we value emotions as guides, then we create an attuned culture of emotional growth. The key is to embrace our feelings and the wisdom within them. In the next chapter, you will be asked to delve deeper into your relationship with your emotions in order to help overcome roadblocks to growth. For now, I would like you to reflect on the lyrics in a song from Red Grammer's *Hello World* CD:

When I Get a Feeling

When I get a feeling, I try to feel it.
I want to know what it is.
What it is trying to say.
Whether I am reeling or quietly feeling.
It's a part of me. I was made that way.

Hello anger you sure look mad.
Hello blues why you feeling so sad?
Anxious, grateful, eager, afraid,
These are just a few of the friends.

Frustrated tells me it is time to relax.
Thoughtful quietly gives me the facts.
Tired tells me to get some rest.
Satisfied says you done your best.

It is time we begin the process of befriending our feelings. It is time we consciously realize that our emotions are truly our feeling buddies.

Chapter

Awareness:
Our Relationship With Our Emotions and How It Affects the Children in Our Lives

Is there a relationship between your credit card bill and your emotions? Do you treat yourself with excess when you feel good, punish yourself with deprivation when you feel bad, attempt to soothe guilt and discomfort with "stuff" or lean on alcohol in an attempt to escape the whole mess? Unless we consciously choose to increase our emotional wellbeing through self-regulation, the cracks in our emotional foundation may leave us addicted to food, our partners, television, our children, exercise, work, prescription pills, social media, sugar, shopping, online gaming, alcohol or drugs, just to name a few. These addictions pave the way for us to subconsciously hand down similar issues to our children. This handing down process doesn't necessarily happen because our children see us knee-deep in addiction, but because they experience us avoiding and artificially managing our emotions. They cannot develop their own healthy skills if they do not see us addressing our emotions in healthy ways.

> Children cannot develop healthy self-regulatory skills unless they see adults consistently addressing their own emotions in healthy ways.

Check the statements you can relate to:

☐   On some level, I believe the right things, situations and people can make me happy.

☐   I am chronically judgmental and critical of others and myself.

☐   No matter how much I would like to deny it, I am governed by the approval of others.

☐   I try so hard to be good, but it seems like life keeps kicking me in the gut.

☐   Deep down, I don't trust myself to make wise decisions.

☐   I know better, but often find it hard to do better.

☐   The best offense is a good defense, yet I still feel out of control.

☐   I often think that other people, businesses and situations should be different.

☐   Getting close to others is scary. One of my biggest fears is hurting those I love or being hurt by them.

☐   I try to control others, keep hidden agendas and try to get others (and life) to go my way as often as possible.

As I read this list, about half of it still hits too close for comfort. If you feel similarly, that's a signal that your emotional wellbeing needs a tune-up or possibly a major overhaul due to adaptations you made to insure survival when you were young.

We are born seeking sustenance outside ourselves for survival. During the early childhood years, we rely on others to meet all of our needs. Others feed us, dress us, love us and teach us how to behave. Survival is the goal of these first bonds. These early bonds become the blueprint for building relationships with others for the rest of our lives (Szalavitz & Perry, 2010).

Think back to when you were a child. What were your parents' responses to your emotions? Did they name, acknowledge and use them as a teaching tool? "You seem angry. You were hoping to stay up later. It's time for bed. You can handle this." Or did they ignore, punish or bribe the feelings away? "Get in that bed. Don't make me have to get up to tell you again." Our relationship with our emotions starts early and can last a lifetime. Some of us learned our angry outbursts brought disappointment or the silent treatment from those we love. Others learned that angry outbursts brought an even greater outburst of anger from adults. Either way, we learned anger was something bad, not simply an internal indication to change. If we are to foster emotional wellbeing within children, we must make the necessary changes to tune up our own systems.

Becoming consciously aware of our current emotional literacy is not a matter of blaming our parents. They certainly did the best they could, as their parents did before them. Think of it this way: When our great-grandparents went to the family doctor, a certain treatment was prescribed. Given today's knowledge, this treatment might appear inappropriate; however, at the time, it was the best treatment known. (I am certainly more willing to take antibiotics than have leeches drain out infection.) The medical profession is willing to reflect on its strategies, gain additional information and make changes. The same must be true for teaching and parenting: Given today's knowledge, past discipline techniques might appear inappropriate, but they were the best we knew at the time. We must simply be willing to reflect on these strategies, gain additional information and make changes.

Conscious awareness of our emotions can drive wonderful changes, bringing us closer to one another. As we become more aware, we heal old wounds and empower our own brilliance instead of relying on early conditioned reactions passed down through the generations. The model our family members provide when handling feelings and the way they interact during emotional moments provides the first school for emotional learning. See if you can relate to the family interactions with Mike, Barb and Kelvin.

Mike and Barb are showing their six-year-old, Kelvin, how to play an educational matching game on the new computer. As Kelvin starts to play, both parents are eager to "help."

"Click the button on the right, on the right, Kelvin!" Mike says, irritated, covering Kelvin's hand over the touchpad and moving the cursor to a button.

Barb reaches over, removes her husband's hand and points to the screen, "Mike, that's not how you turn the cards over. It's over here. Kelvin, now click here. See? Over here."

Kelvin bites his lip and pulls his hand away from the touchpad.

"Kelvin, pay attention. We are trying to help you! Do you want to learn the game or not? Click this button, remember the card and then click the other button, try again." Kelvin timidly puts his hand back on the touchpad and starts clicking any button. "Kelvin, you're clicking the wrong button."

Mike rolls his eyes, "Stop, stop! What's the matter with you? It is not that difficult."

Barb says, "Just leave everything alone and watch me. I'll show you how to play. Move over."

Kelvin, unable to please his parents or play the game, stands up and his mom slides into the seat he just occupied. His parents start bickering. "Barb, you're doing exactly what Kelvin did. No wonder he's slow." Kelvin blinks as his eyes fill with tears.

"Shut up, Mike. You can't even turn the computer on properly, much less help with the game," retorts Barb. Neither parent seems to notice the tear roll down Kelvin's cheek.

Children learn deep lessons about life, emotions and relationships from moments like these. One simple conclusion Kelvin could draw from this exchange is that his parents don't care about his feelings. By default, he might also think they don't care about him. He may begin to confuse helping others with controlling others. He may begin to believe he is the cause of his parents' discord. When similar moments are repeated countless times over the course of childhood, they impart fundamental emotional messages that can last a lifetime. These lessons, albeit unconscious, are so powerful that they can determine our life course.

Karen was the mom of two girls active in soccer. She was the designated driver for taking four girls to soccer practice twice a week. Karen found other drivers irritating, billboards distracting and noise in the car overwhelming. She acted out her emotions through judgment and sarcasm. As she drove the girls around town, she gave a running commentary on what's wrong with the roads, the signs, and how others should drive, act and dress.

"Look at the way that teen drives. No one in the car is even wearing seat belts. He's going to kill everyone in his car and take out a few more. Do you think he cares? No, all of them only care about having fun and joy riding. Selfish little jerks!"

Then a bit later, "What was that? I guess he doesn't have a blinker in his car. He would rather cut me off than care enough to put on a blinker."

Still more, "See these signs? Look at all the junk they're trying to sell us. It's all propaganda to brainwash us into more, more and more. I'm glad we aren't stupid enough to buy into that nonsense."

Karen is teaching the girls that it's acceptable to act out frustration by judging, criticizing, blaming and using sarcasm. The sad part is that when her girls feel frustrated and express themselves in the same ways she has modeled, she will most likely admonish them for being disrespectful.

Recent research indicates the way parents treat each other is even more powerful for a child than the way the parents treat the child (Szalavitz & Perry,

2010). Some parents are emotionally gifted and others behave atrociously. Emotionally intelligent parents are an enormous benefit to children (Goleman, 1995). Recent research shows:

> Recent research indicates the way parents treat each other is even more powerful for a child than the way the parents treat the child.
>
> – Szalavitz & Perry, 2010

- Children with emotional and social competence are more successful in school and in the work place. Emotional health equals optimal brain development.

- Helping children manage upset feelings is a form of disease prevention. The toxicity of poorly managed feelings is on par with how smoking cigarettes contributes to poor health.

- Children who learn to manage and express their emotions create healthier relationships.

Since social pressures are no longer the glue that holds a marriage together, then the emotional competencies between a husband and wife become crucial skills. Research indicates couples that were more emotionally competent in their marriage were also more effective in helping children manage their feelings in healthy ways (Katz & Gottman, 1994).

In short, parents with high levels of emotional wellbeing who have access to their Emotional Guidance Systems (EGS) tend to raise smart, healthy, happy children who love and care for themselves and others. On the other hand, the outcome for children without access to their EGS is staggering in terms of depression, addiction, dropping out of school, bullying, violence and abusive relationships.

At this point, some of you may think, "Wow, parents need to get their act together!" Well the same is true for teachers. Home may be the first "school" for emotional learning, but school is the second. Each of us has a unique relationship with our own feelings. It shows up in triggered moments at school, just like at home. The social-emotional skills educators model and their level of emotional wellbeing has a tremendous impact on a child's development and academic success.

When I ask teachers all over the world if they believe their inner state dictates their behavior, the overwhelming response is, "Yes!" Teachers see the relationship between their own inner states and their willingness to be cooperative, kind and caring. Yet, when it comes to discipline, nearly every one focuses solely on a child's behavior. "I don't have time to acknowledge their internal states; I must stop problem behaviors and focus on academics!" We claim we don't have the moment it takes to help an upset child access a higher internal state in order to make permanent behavioral changes. I suspect, however, that we simply don't know how. The tools in this book lead us through the process so we can raise our level of emotional wellbeing and teach children to do the same. In this way, we can achieve maximum learning in all classrooms. As one child so aptly put it, "It's hard to focus on math when your parents are getting a divorce."

Whether we are parents or educators (or both), we must stop placing blame on our past, stop making excuses and stop avoiding our emotions. The remainder of this chapter focuses on the adaptations we have developed that distance us from our feelings and impede our emotional wellbeing. It may be a difficult journey at times, but it is one we are safe to undertake and completely capable of handling. Embrace the opportunity to look within and begin healing your emotional self so you can effectively teach emotional wellbeing to the children in your care.

Primary and Secondary Systems

Many of us have two layers of emotions. These can be called primary and secondary. The primary emotions are uncomplicated, natural responses that are innately fundamental to human functioning (Spradlin, 2003). When we allow them into our consciousness, they can complete their integrative function as intended. When a dear friend arrives for a long-overdue visit, we erupt with happiness. When a beloved pet passes away, we cry to express the sadness of our loss. When someone jumps out from behind a tree and yells, "Boo," fear grabs our attention as we startle and hold our breath. When we work endless hours on a project and our boss complicates it with new instructions, anger emerges because our personal goals are thwarted. These are our natural tendencies.

Emotion researchers are not unanimous in determining how many primary emotions exist. Ekman (2003) describes our primary emotions as scared, sad, angry, happy, surprised and disgusted. In this book and the *Feeling Buddies Self-Regulation Toolkits*, I use four primary emotions of angry, sad, scared and happy, and their four related "cousins" of frustration, disappointed, anxious and calm.

Secondary emotions are considered "secondary" because they are not necessarily related to an innate survival response in a given situation. They are tied to a story or adaptive belief we have embraced as truth. They come in behind the primary emotions and are experienced through perceptual filters we have created.

Secondary emotions are the outcome of the adaptations we believed we needed to make in our families of origin in order to survive. They are feelings about emotions. An example would be feeling shame about feeling sad. We unconsciously foster this secondary layer of emotions by telling children how they are feeling or should be feeling. You might learn to feel shame about feeling sad if adults often said things like this around you: "You should be ashamed of yourself for carrying on this way. The dog is dead. There's nothing we can do about that. Now pull yourself together."

Secondary emotions are recorded on our personal CD-Rom, which is created through unconscious family conditioning and passed down from generation to generation. They consist of judgments, assumptions and unexamined beliefs, and are *not* our true primary feelings. They only describe how we feel or think about our feelings. They mask our true emotions and make it difficult to accurately name them. Shame, guilt, boredom, humiliation and embarrassment are common secondary feelings: We might feel ashamed of ourselves for feeling angry with an elderly uncle or embarrassed about our happiness over a life success. Primary feelings can also become secondary feelings: We might feel angry with ourselves for feeling afraid to make a presentation in front of our peers. We might feel sad about feeling angry. I know a woman who cries or laughs when she feels angry, scared, sad or happy. Her family allowed crying and laughing as a release from all the primary blocked emotions. So, her secondary emotions for everything are crying or laughing. Additional examples of common secondary emotions are:

- Feeling guilty for feeling happy.
- Feeling anxious for feeling angry.

- Feeling scared for feeling angry.
- Feeling worried about losing happiness.

The chart below shows how we can bury our primary feelings underneath life stories, defenses and secondary feelings.

Defenses
(Story to support and maintain secondary feelings)

| My partner left me because I was unlovable and worthless | My dad loved my sister more because she obeyed better | I lost the job because the boss treated me unfairly | A story from your life |

Secondary Feelings

| Feeling shame about feeling fear | Feeling sad about feeling sad | Feeling guilty about feeling angry |
| Feeling angry about feeling angry | Feeling angry about feeling sad | Feeling anxious about feeling scared |

Primary Emotions

| Angry | Sad | Scared | Happy |

Foundational Experience

| Love Pleasant | Fear Unpleasant |

Five-year-old Maddie is dressing herself, putting one leg into her favorite jeans. Her younger brother, Garrison, runs wildly into her room and pushes her over. Maddie is furious! She chases Garrison into the living room where she suddenly finds herself standing half-naked in front of her mother and a group of neighbors. Her mother, shocked to see Maddie in just her underwear questions, "Maddie, what on earth are you doing?" Without waiting for an answer, she continues, "Don't you see we have company? You are old enough to know better than to run around the house half-naked."

Mom doesn't realize it, but she is blanketing a secondary emotion over Maddie's true feeling of anger toward her brother and any discomfort Maddie might naturally feel about being half-naked in front of guests.

Maddie says, "But Mom, Garrison started it. I hate him. He's a brat and he pushed me."

"Maddie, how dare you talk about your brother like that! We do not call each other names in this family. You are embarrassing yourself and me. Now go to your room and come back fully dressed and behaving pleasantly for company."

Can you see how Maddie's mom is fostering a secondary guidance system that overrides Maddie's own? She attempts to replace Maddie's anger with guilt, demands she ignore her upset and directs her to behave "pleasantly." The situation could have gone completely different if Mom had been able to recognize and regulate her own feelings of fear overlaid with embarrassment. If she had better access to her own EGS, Mom could have responded to Maddie instead of reacted. It might have gone something like this:

Maddie runs into the living room and surprises her mother and house-guests. Mom feels her insides heat up and takes time to realize the embarrassment she feels. Taking a few deep breaths to calm herself, she is able to acknowledge fear of the judgment of others and say, "Maddie you ran in here with you hands balled in a fist and your face like this. You seem angry. Something big must have happened for you to run out in just your underwear! What on earth happened?"

Maddie stops, realizes she's standing half-naked in front of guests and responds, "I was putting on my jeans and Garrison knocked me down. He's a brat!"

Mom, breathing slowly and deeply, says, "How infuriating. It makes total sense that you feel so angry and would run after him."

"Well, yeah. Aren't you going to do something about it?" Maddie asks.

"You bet I will. I will help you talk to Garrison so you can teach him how to respect your room, your things and you. What could you do now to get ready for that?"

"I'm going to put the rest of my clothes on first," Maddie says.

"And if you calm down a bit, Garrison will be better able to hear what you have to say to him," Mom suggests as Maddie returns to her room.

Hopefully, you can feel the difference between the two scenarios. If we, as adults, do not have access to our EGS, we cannot help children learn to listen to theirs. Instead, we drill into them how their behavior is right or wrong, good or bad. We use lecture and "reasoning" to tell them how their behavior has hurt others and will not be tolerated. We attempt to make them feel bad on the inside, hoping they will change on the outside. None of this puts children in touch with their own emotional guidance. Instead, it overrides it with a misguided socialization process. We tell them how they should feel instead of encouraging them to be aware of what they are feeling. We begin to build a secondary system within them that says, "I will tell you how you feel and think, what to feel and think, which feelings and thoughts are allowed, and how to express them. I will be your guidance system, not you." Over time, as adults project thoughts and feelings onto a child, the child creates a secondary external guidance system. This system is based on the mood and emotional state of others, not a child's own internal compass. It teaches the children to make decisions and allow their moral compass to be based on the approval of others instead of encouraging the inner wisdom needed in a given situation.

Uncovering and accurately identifying your primary feelings may seem like you are an archaeologist of your heart. You may be so accustomed to your secondary emotions that digging up your true feelings may seem like long, hard, dirty work. The good news is that no giant boulder is going to come crashing down and no villain is coming to steal what you find. This journey is yours alone to undertake, and you are perfectly safe to take it. You must uncover these feelings because your primary feelings are the only ones that are real. Primary feelings are your natural guidance system whose sole purpose is to remind you who you are and guide you back to happiness, our natural state. I often encourage myself or my friends who simply do not have a clue as to what they are feeling to just choose one of the primary four: angry, scared, sad or happy. If I find myself ruminating in my head about who did what to whom, I say, "Becky, just find a feeling word." If it is secondary word like "guilty," I say, "Try again. Choose one of the four primary emotions of angry, sad, scared and happy."

Most of us find it hard to believe that feelings are the "good guys." We have thought of feelings as "bad guys," because they have been used as an excuse to attack, abandon or belittle. Watching our parents act out their unconscious inner states was often a painful experience. As a result, we developed a secondary guidance system, we created protective personality responses (turning ourselves into pleasers, controllers and clowns), and we learned to hide our feelings in an effort to deaden ourselves from the hurt in order to feel safe. If we want the children in our care to grow up with true emotional wellbeing rather than an extensive list of false coping strategies, it's time for us to acknowledge, accurately name, befriend and learn how to regulate our own feelings.

Four Emotionally Unhealthy Teaching and Parenting Styles

Our relationship with our emotions dictates the type of empathy and discipline we offer ourselves and children. The voice we use internally when we talk to ourselves is the same voice we use with children when we encounter a difficult situation. Often, it is not the kindest voice. I frequently hear the voice in my head say, "Becky, what were you thinking?" I utter the same words when I feel stressed and a child has made a simple mistake: "Deborah, what were you thinking?" This criticism of myself and others covers my underlying frustration with the world not going my way. The key is to notice the way the voice in our head attempts to govern us, and understand that unless we become conscious of our emotions, we will approach children in the same ways.

The four most common emotionally unhealthy teaching and parenting styles are ignoring, dismissing, punishing, and fixing/saving. These styles are not necessarily a global approach to all feelings. In my family, anger was punished, scared was ignored and sadness was perfectly acceptable for me (as a female) but an unacceptable feeling for my brother.

Ignoring: If we generally deny our own feelings, we will deny or ignore children's feelings. We may not even notice their feelings as we continue with the academic or household needs of the moment. We will offer little or no empathy to children or ourselves. This style of dealing with feelings is called "ignoring." This style emerged as we experienced situations like the one below during our early years:

Child:	Head down, tears running down the cheeks, approaches mom and says, "Because her dad lost his job, my best friend is moving to North Carolina. I'll never see her again."
Mom:	"Did you finish your homework? We need to leave this house in three seconds or I will be late to work!"

Dismissing: If we tend to minimize or dismiss our own feelings, we will tend to dismiss the feelings of the children in our care. This style asks us to compare our feeling state with those worse off than ourselves or doing fine in similar situations, and discount or minimize our need to feel the way we do. Using the same example, dismissing would sound like the following:

> **Child:** Head down, tears running down the cheeks, approaches mom and says, "Because her dad lost his job, my best friend is moving to North Carolina. I'll never see her again."
>
> **Mom:** "For heaven's sake, that's just silly. With all this technology, you can't lose anyone. Your father lost his job and he's still here."

Punishing: If we have an antagonistic relationship with our emotions, we will tend to punish ourselves for what we are feeling and punish children who show emotion in the classroom or home. Those of us who get mad at ourselves because "it's stupid to feel this way" also become irritated by children's feelings. This style of dealing with feelings is called "punishing." Using the same example from above, punishing would sound like this:

> **Child:** Head down, tears running down the cheeks, approaches mom and says, "Because her dad lost his job, my best friend is moving to North Carolina. I'll never see her again."
>
> **Mom:** "Your drama is so annoying. Stop whining or I'll give you something real to complain about. Go get your room cleaned, NOW!"

Fixing/Saving: The fourth most common way of handling feelings is saving or fixing them. If we turn to food, shopping or special privileges to medicate our feelings, then we will do the same with children's. If we tend to worry that our feelings are so strong they will overwhelm us, we will want to save our children from their discomfort. This style of dealing with feelings is called "fixing/saving." The same example demonstrates this:

> **Child:** Head down, tears running down the cheeks, approaches mom and says, "Because her dad lost his job, my best friend is moving to North Carolina. I'll never see her again."
>
> **Mom:** "Oh honey. I'll make sure you see each other. I'll contact her mother and take care of everything for you two. It will get better. For now, let's go out for some ice cream."

Fixing/saving children from the experience of feeling the emotional distress of anger, sadness or fear is extremely common. Saving involves preventing the internal discomfort of feelings, while fixing tries to remedy the discomfort after the fact. "Saving" children from their feelings also "saves" them from the awareness that they are in charge of their inner state and behavior. Feelings house our power and our responsibility. When we seek to save children from their feelings, we also put ourselves in charge of their feelings and inner state. They grow up believing other people are in charge of their feelings, and the only way to have peace of mind is for other people to change. Fixing or saving children from their feelings prevents them from accessing the natural emotional guidance that comes from experiencing internal distress, remorse, disappointment or angst from making poor choices. Without the opportunity to learn, they will continue to make poor choices in a process of escalation that can (and often does) lead to life or death moments.

A friend of mine kept saving her child from experiencing discomfort at school. She would demand her little girl be moved into different classes, have grades changed and have exceptions made so she wouldn't experience tough feelings like disappointment. This continued throughout elementary and into middle school. In high school, the girl fell in love with a boy who ultimately broke her heart. Lacking the skills to deal with her overwhelming emotions, the girl killed herself. Learning how to tolerate the discomfort generated from anger, sadness, fear or happiness is a life or death lesson.

Activity

The following activity will help you understand your relationship with your emotions more clearly. Look at the images below and reflect on how the four primary feelings of angry, sad, scared and happy relate to the following questions:

- How did **your parents** handle you when you felt angry (acting out, stomping your feet, throwing a fit), when you felt sad (crying, whining or sulking), when you felt scared (hiding, refusing to try, asking for help) or happy (jumping up and down, giggling and laughing)?
- Recall a specific situation in your upbringing that relates to each feeling. Examples: A friend moved to another town. You wanted something and were told "no." You were selected to the varsity soccer team.
- Recall the words you were told, the tone of voice and the facial expression that carried all the information.
- Place a check in the box that best represents the emotional style your parents used with you as a child for each core emotion.

Style of Upbringing	Angry	Sad	Scared	Happy
Ignoring				
Dismissing				
Punishing				
Fixing / Saving				

Next, think about a present day moment when you experienced each of these emotions as an adult.

- What do you tend to say to **yourself** or unconsciously do when the world does not go your way? When you have had a loss such as a job, a raise, a dear friend? What do you tend to say to yourself or do when you feel anxious or scared about an upcoming event? What do you say or do when you feel happy or are celebrating your happiness? Recall the words you say in your head and the tone you use with yourself.
- Put a check in the box that best represents the emotional style you find yourself using with yourself during emotional moments.

Style with Adult Self	Angry	Sad	Scared	Happy
Ignoring				
Dismissing				
Punishing				
Fixing / Saving				

Now, think of a recent encounter with a child when he or she was experiencing each of the core emotions of angry, sad, scared and happy.

- How did **you respond to the child** when he or she was acting out in anger? What about when he or she was crying uncontrollably, scared to try something or gleefully happy?
- Recall the words you used and the tone of your voice.
- Place a check in the box that best describes the emotional style you think you are using with your children or the children in your care.

Style with the Children in Your Care	Angry	Sad	Scared	Happy
Ignoring				
Dismissing				
Punishing				
Fixing / Saving				

Are you beginning to see a correlation between how you were raised, what you say to yourself with your inner speech, and how you handle certain behaviors and emotions with children?

Many of you may be thinking, "But I've been dealing with my emotions that way for as long as I can remember! If I don't ignore them, rant and rave about them, beat myself up for having them, or take them out for a hot fudge sundae, what do I do with them?"

There is a healthy alternative: coaching the five-step self-regulation process. This coaching process begins with befriending your feelings and learning how to coach yourself through those feelings. You then learn how to coach children through their feelings. Remember, your relationship with your emotions dictates the way you will interact with children as they experience and act out their emotions. The same self-regulation techniques that assist you will serve the children's emotional growth.

The Story

Primary emotions serve us well. Secondary emotions keep us stuck in a story or belief that is deeply false, hurtful to all parties involved, and results in emotionally unhealthy parenting and teaching styles. If you have trouble seeing if you are stuck, just listen to your friends. Some of your friends have been telling the same story for years about how they have been wronged, victimized or abandoned. They are stuck in a story that is not true and cannot change. Change occurs by pulling the primary emotions from the story and allowing them to rise to consciousness to deliver a wonderful message. This message is your guidance and will allow you to reframe your story, upgrading it with positive intent for yourself and others. The new upgraded story is closer to the truth and leads us back to our core state of loving wholeness.

We all carry around stories from our past. One of my stories involves my parents who both had Alzheimer's. About nine years ago, my mother was in the moderate stages of Alzheimer's. She also had emphysema and heart problems. My dad was in the beginning stages of Alzheimer's, incapable of remembering enough to understand the nature and severity of Mom's problems. He was furiously protective of her and demanded he would care for her, give her medication and oversee the oxygen she required. As much as he believed he was capable of providing these services for her, he was not. My story was, "My father is going to kill my mother." My anger toward him grew as months and years passed, as did my fear about my mother's comfort and survival. The angrier I became, the more evidence I collected that my story was true. I would fight with my brother, trying to convince him the truth of my story. Ultimately, I became willing to pull my primary feelings out of the story. My deep sadness for the loss of my parents' mental health and my fear that someday I may be in the same situation were real. The story and the secondary emotions of anger, guilt and shame were false. Once I was willing to do this, I was able to regulate my sadness and my fear enough to make healthier decisions for my parents and myself. It also healed my relationship with my brother.

We must learn to listen to our primary feelings. Listening to our feelings requires we become aware of them. We must be cognizant of what they feel like in our bodies, look like on our faces and sound like in our tone of voice. We must learn the language of feelings so we can hear the messages they send. The next chapter begins to expand your awareness of your feelings. Most of us can only identify two inner states, "I'm fine" and "I'm upset." It is time to broaden and deepen our awareness of our feelings.

Listen to Your Feelings is the music CD created to accompany this book and the *Feeling Buddies Self-Regulation Toolkits*. It consists of 29 songs that help children name and tame their emotions. I designed the CD for children, but think it is essential in helping adults listen to their feelings, too.

Chapter

Feeling Messages:
Following Our Emotional Guidance System

Our Emotional Guidance System (EGS) allows our feelings to communicate with us. Our feelings have embedded messages that steer us to continually return to our optimal state of love. Just as physical pain nudges us to say, "Pay attention, something is going on," our feelings do the same thing. If we ignore the messages of pain or the messages of our feelings, potential catastrophes could lie ahead. We have all read about the jogger, apparently in perfect health, who drops dead of a heart attack while running. The body had been sending out signals before this moment, but they went unnoticed by the jogger. My neighbor, Mike, had something in his left foot for forty-four years. One day the pain became so great he had trouble walking. X-rays indicated a tiny glass shard in his foot. During the ensuing surgery, the surgeon found Mike's foot to be infected so badly that a marble-sized clump of tissue had died and turned black. Just as the shard in Mike's foot eventually destroyed tissue, the buried disappointment of a five-year-old can lead to relationship sabotage later in life.

We must listen to our feelings and to their guidance. In order to do this, we must first be aware they exist and allow them to communicate with us. This is a tall order for many of us. Recently, I fasted for ten days. Many people kept asking me, "Aren't you hungry?" Surprisingly, the answer was, "No." Instead, the fasting led me to an increased awareness of buried feelings bubbling to the surface. I had been medicating these feelings with food for years. Without the food, they were right in my face. Specifically, I felt intense sadness about my parents' Alzheimer's and deep grief about my inability to bear children. With this newfound awareness, I worked hard those ten days to feel my feelings rather than become my emotions. Instead of repeating the habit of stiff-arming my emotions, I befriended them, named them and allowed myself to be gently guided into a new perception. As a side effect of my attempt for a healthier body, my mind is now healthier, too.

What are your feelings trying to tell you? What are children's feelings telling them and us? How can we use these messages to improve all of our relationships, stay on track to achieve our goals and stay in touch with the best of who we are? Many feelings have common themes and messages. If we are aware of these themes and messages then we are better able to fine tune our ability to hear them. As mentioned in Chapter 2, most of us focus on the behavior when we approach conflict. We tend to ask questions such as, "What were you doing?" or "Who had it first?" instead of addressing the inner state. Conscious Discipline asks you to address the inner state first and the behavior second using the following DNA (**D**escribe, **N**ame, **A**cknowledge) process:

> **Describe:** "Your arm went backward like this." Describe and mirror the emotional signals the child's body and face are providing. "Describing" means verbally capturing the moment without judgment. If a camera could capture an image showing what you've said, you are describing the moment. If not, you are most likely judging the moment. "Mirroring" is demonstrating the child's movements and expressions, and will usually bring the child's gaze to you. When the child looks at you, take a deep calming breath to cut the intensity of the moment.

> **Name:** Name the feeling being communicated. "You seem angry." Name the feeling using your best educated guess.

> **Acknowledge:** End the process by acknowledging the child's positive

intent and desire. "You wanted _____" or "You were hoping _____." Acknowledge the child's most heartfelt wishes.

The DNA process enables us to deal with the emotional state first and the behavior second. Our awareness of children's states is key to the DNA process and to encouraging emotional regulation. If we are preoccupied with what to cook for dinner or the supplies we'll need for the science lesson, then we are going to miss all the facial and body signals that point us toward helping children self-regulate. Conscious Discipline helps adults become present in the moment, ensuring that disciplining children is possible. One of the reasons we coach adults to describe and mirror the child's face during times of upset is because this requires the adult to attune (be present) with the child. Describing and mirroring do two things:

1. They help the child become aware of her own face and other body signals, and thus the faces and signals of others experiencing the same emotion.

2. They help the adult stay in the present moment, thus accessing the higher centers of the brain. From here, the adult is able to offer guidance from a compassionate heart.

We will build on this DNA process in a variety of contexts as we pursue the five-step process. First, however, we must learn what each emotion is saying. Every emotion has involuntary facial and vocal signals that help us distinguish one from another. These facial and vocal signals are beyond our conscious control and serve to nonverbally communicate our inner states to others. The key is for us to become conscious of these signals, which leads to accurately naming the feeling and hearing its message. Recognizing these unconscious signals and messages is essential if we are to guide children in making sense of their emotions and expressing them in healthy, socially appropriate ways.

The eight emotions we will explore are: Angry and its cousin, Frustration. Scared and its cousin, Anxious. Sad and its cousin, Disappointed. Happy and its cousin, Calm.

The Primary Emotion Anger and Its Cousin, Frustration

The theme of anger is that someone or something is getting in the way of what we are intent on doing, achieving or possessing. The more our goal is thwarted, the greater the degree of anger that is generated. The more we believe our goals are deliberately being blocked, the more intense the anger. One of the most dangerous features of this emotion is that anger calls forth more intense anger and the cycle can rapidly escalate (Ekman, 2003).

The message of anger has two parts: "Calm down and change." The first part, calming down, is needed to stop the impending, rapidly escalating cycle. Once calmness is achieved, the next message is a gentle nudge to change. The change needed may be a change in location, a change in friendships, a change of perception, a change in action, or to rewrite an old life script or story. Often when we become angry, our misguided goal is to get the other person or situation to change so we can continue with our own personal agenda. We demand they change, do things differently and remove the blockage that, in our mind, is getting in the way of our success and/or happiness. When we learn how to move from "I am angry" to "I feel my anger," the truth becomes more apparent: We are getting in our own way.

Frustration can also generate anger. The theme of frustration, though similar to anger, is different in intensity and source. We tend to blame our anger on something we perceive another person or situation has done to us or caused us to do. Frustration, on the other hand, is generally about our own shortcomings. It is related to our failure to achieve our desired goal. A classic example with a two-year-old is when she insists, "Me do it," only to become frustrated to discover she can't do it alone. Once the child becomes frustrated, it is our job to help her feel the frustration, name it and ultimately reframe it in order to solve the problem.

Frustration is about our lack of skill in a certain area. Often we project our frustrations, like anger, onto others. Here is a wonderful activity: Write down all the things that irritate you about a significant other, a boss or a child. Then leave the list alone for a while. Come back to the list and, just for fun, assume the list is about you. What do you discover? Often, the irritations you felt about the other person are really frustrations you feel about yourself. Frustration's message says, "Calm down and patiently see or do things differently." Projecting your frustration onto shoes that are difficult to tie or old golf clubs that are keeping you off the PGA Tour are deeply ingrained beliefs. Frustration's message is that tying your shoes or hitting that golf ball requires more patience and more practice.

I often find myself becoming frustrated when I am ready to go and the people I'm going with are not ready. For years I avoided this frustration by being the last one ready or arriving fashionably late. That strategy allowed me to stay calm and present without ruining the event with my crankiness. The downside was that I did not consider the impact my lateness had on others. My frustration came from an early family dynamic. My mother would prepare dinner for the family and my father would show up late. My mother, brother and I could not eat until my father arrived. Once he sat down at the table, dinner was cold and the atmosphere was deeply unpleasant as my parents argued and condemned one another. I would sit as quiet as a mouse, anxiously praying for them to stop arguing. Looking back, I can see my frustration was overlaid with anxiety. Anxiety blocked the energy of frustration from coming into my awareness. This left me stuck in an intolerable state of distress for many years. Once I was able to access the frustration that was hidden under the anxiety and could feel the emotion, I could allow the gentle message, "Calm down and see things differently," emerge. This gave me the opportunity to develop new strategies. Now I can wait by simply asking, "How long do you think it will be before you are ready?" With this information, I can easily regulate my anxiety and see the situation through my current eyes instead of the eyes of a five-year-old Becky.

Coaching Anger and Its Cousin, Frustration

When we see anger in children, we can approach and coach:

> **Step 1:** Coach the child to calm by taking a few deep breaths.
> Be a S.T.A.R. (**S**mile, **T**ake a deep breath, **A**nd **R**elax.)

Step 2: Help the child move from "I am angry" to "I feel angry." "Your face is going like this (demonstrate). You seem angry."

Step 3: Help the child begin the change process. "You wanted the marker. You may not grab. When you want the marker say, *May I have a turn?*"

Sound familiar? Steps two and three of this coaching process are the same as in the DNA (**D**escribe, **N**ame, **A**cknowledge) process described earlier.

When we see frustration in a child, we can approach and coach:

Step 1: Coach the child to calm by taking a few deep breaths. Be a S.T.A.R. (**S**mile, **T**ake a deep breath, **A**nd **R**elax.)

Step 2: Help the child move from "I am frustrated" to "I feel frustrated." "Your face is going like this (demonstrate). You seem frustrated."

Step 3: Offer a new perspective or strategy. "You seem to be having trouble tying your shoe. Who could you ask for help?"

Do you see the coaching pattern for both angry and frustration?

Calm down = Be a S.T.A.R.
Change = Apply the DNA process

Recognizing Anger in Yourself and Others

When we become angry, sensations shoot through our body. Feelings of pressure, tension and heat occur. This is where the expression "hot under the collar" originated. Your heart rate increases, as does respiration and blood pressure. Your face tends to get red and there is an impulse to move toward the target of the anger. This is why angry children will often come after us. When you become angry, there is a tendency to bite down hard, upper teeth against lower teeth, and to thrust the chin forward. If you are speaking, your voice becomes louder with a harsh tone as your vocal cords tense. In anger, the blood flow increases to your hands, making them warm and preparing them to strike, shake, throw or hit the object of the anger. Most of these emotional expressions last about four seconds and some are as short as a half a second (Ekman, 2003). Most of us can identify these nonverbal and verbal cues in that short amount of time when they come from others. It is part of our survival system. It is much more difficult to become aware of them in ourselves. This is why other people generally know what we are feeling before we do!

Take a moment and think back to a time you felt so angry you wanted to hit someone. If that has never happened, try to remember a time when you felt so angry your voice got loud and you said things you later regretted. See if, in hindsight, you can recall the inner sensations related to anger. Can you feel the pressure? Can you feel the tension? Where is it in your body? What do you feel? Take a moment to really experience this activity. It is important to know as soon as possible when you are becoming angry because your awareness will allow you to calm down enough to feel it, name it and reframe it. The same is true for children.

Angry
"Calm down and change."

Frustrated
"Calm down and patiently see or
do things differently."

Many parents share with me that if they walk away from their angry children, the children come after them. Ginny Luther, one of our Loving Guidance Associates, tells a wonderful story about her two sons Bart and Nick. Bart was a handful from birth. He had a difficult temperament and was determined to have the world go his way at all costs. Nick had an easy temperament and wanted to please. One day Ginny was furious with three-year-old Bart's behavior. She began to yell, "That's it. I've had it. I am no longer your mother. My name is now George." With that, Ginny ran to her room and slammed the door to keep herself and her children safe from her escalating anger. Nick followed her crying, "You can't be George. You're my Mommy. I want my Mommy!" Bart, following on Nick's heels, banged on the door yelling, "George, come out here NOW!"

The Primary Emotion Scared and Its Cousin, Anxious

Scared is the 911 of emotions. The theme of scared is about the threat of physical or psychological harm, whether it be real or imagined. There is no question many of us fear things that, in fact, pose no danger. A good example of this is a child's fear of the dark or my fear of cows. (Yes, cows.) The most common response to feeling scared is to freeze or flee. If we do not freeze or flee, the next most common response is to feel angry and attack whatever threatened us. We often feel these two emotions, scared and angry, in rapid succession. The message of the emotion scared is, "Help me feel safe and protected."

When a person becomes scared, the autonomic nervous system is activated and responds immediately without conscious prompting. The brain sends out signals to the muscles and internal organs to prepare for an emergency. The heart beats faster to deliver more oxygen to the body in preparation for a response similar to that of anger. However, when feeling scared, the blood goes to the large muscles in the legs, making the hands colder (instead of warmer as when feeling angry) and prepares the body to flee. The breathing rate increases, sweat glands increase production and hormones, like adrenalin, are released into the bloodstream. This reaction is essential as a protective mechanism, preparing our bodies for "fight or flight."

Anxiety, like fear, is also a warning signal to let us know of potential or impending danger. The difference between scared and anxious is that scared is a response to a threat that is known, while anxiety is a response to a threat that is unknown. Both are about safety. A classic example is how parents of teenagers feel when the child comes home later than the designated curfew. While he is missing, his parents' anxiety is almost unbearable. When he arrives, that anxiety can morph into anger at warp speed, and we loudly lecture the child who was so precious moments ago. Anxiety is something we anticipate in our mind, which we perceive to be uncontrollable or unavoidable. The message of anxiety is, "Breathe deeply, focus on the present and get more information."

Consider this statistic: One in approximately 40 million Americans age 18 or older is in an activated fight or flight state when there is no direct threat present. That translates to 18 percent of us who are triggered by feeling anxious at any one time (Kessler, Chiu, Demler, & Walters, 2005). It's essential we add some new self-regulatory skills to our repertoire.

Coaching Scared and Its Cousin, Anxious

We can approach children who are scared by reassuring them of our authority and our commitment to their safety. Again, we approach and coach:

> **Step 1:** Breathe to calm your own arousal state.
> Be a S.T.A.R. (**S**mile, **T**ake a deep breath, **A**nd **R**elax.)
>
> **Step 2:** Help the child move from "I am scared" to "I feel scared."
> "Your face is going like this (demonstrate). You seem scared. You're safe. Breathe with me. I will keep you safe. Keep breathing."
>
> **Step 3:** Keep your commitment to emotional, physical and spiritual safety. Physically comfort the child.

We can approach children who are anxious by reassuring them of our authority and our commitment to their safety, as well as offer strategies to acquire additional information. Approach and coach:

Step 1: Breathe to calm your own arousal state. Be a S.T.A.R. (**S**mile, **T**ake a deep breath, **A**nd **R**elax.) Notice the child's nonverbal cues.

Step 2: Help the child move from "I am anxious" to "I feel anxious." "Your face is going like this (demonstrate). You seem anxious. You're safe. Breathe with me. What would help you feel safer?"

Step 3: Suggest ways to obtain present time information.

The Difference Between Scared and Its Cousin, Anxious

Because "scared" is for more tangible threats and "anxious" is more freefloating in nature, we must approach and coach a child using slightly different DNA words.

Helping a child who seems scared:

Describe: "Your eyes are going like this. Your mouth is going like this."

Name: "You seem scared."

Acknowledge: "Beth, you're safe. Breathe with me. I will keep you safe."

Helping a child who seems anxious:

Describe: "Your eyes are going like this. Your mouth is going like this."

Name: "Breathe with me. You seem anxious."

Acknowledge: "Let's go look at the schedule together to see when your mom will be back."

Recognizing Fear in Yourself and Others

The facial expression of fear includes the widening of the eyes (out of anticipation of what will happen next), the dilation of the pupils (to take in more light), the upper lip rising, the brows drawing together and the lips stretching horizontally (Ohman, 2000).

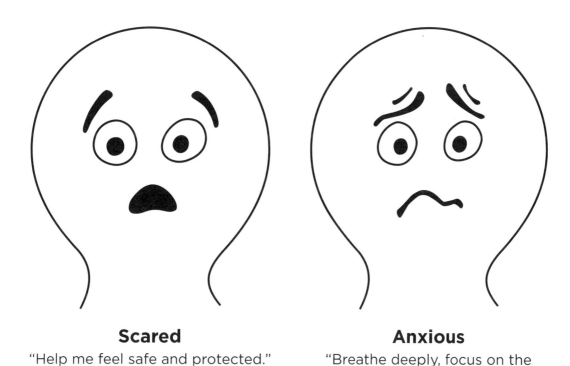

Scared
"Help me feel safe and protected."

Anxious
"Breathe deeply, focus on the present, get more information."

The next time you become aware you are feeling scared, take some deep breaths and get help from a trusted source. Notice the sources that come to your mind. The next time you are experiencing anxiety, take some calming breaths and check the truth of your inner speech. Ask yourself, "Is it true that if I don't get my paperwork in by Monday, I will lose my job?"

The Primary Emotion Sadness and Its Cousin, Disappointment

In anger, there is an impulse to move closer to the target of the anger. In fear, there is an impulse to freeze. In sadness, there is no impulse for action. The theme of sadness is about the loss of something that you value. The more you value what you lost, the deeper the sadness.

In sadness, there is an overall loss of muscle tone and posture slumps in withdrawal. There is a tendency to look down or stare into space. Over time, movements and even thought processes slow down. In this inactive state, the levels of the neurotransmitters serotonin and noradrenalin are reduced. The reduction of these chemicals increases our sadness, creating a cycle that can lead to clinical depression if left unchecked. The message of sadness is, "Seek comfort from those you love." It is a signal to our social support network that we are calling out for comfort. With one in 10 people over the age of six taking anti-depressants, helping children deal with loss is an essential skill for parents and teachers (Olfson & Marcus, 2009).

Disappointment is felt when our hopes and expectations do not materialize. If we do not feel and process our disappointment, it can easily and quickly turn into anger or sadness. The message of disappointment is, "Keep breathing, I can handle this."

When I was nine years old, I pleaded loudly with Santa Claus for a guitar, hoping my parents would overhear the request. Already aware that the man whose lap I sat on was not really Santa, I needed to cover all my bases. Later that day, I made sure my parents knew how important that guitar was to me by talking about it incessantly. When Christmas morning arrived, I tore into a box that looked like it might contain a guitar, but actually held a ukulele. Disappointment enveloped my body. I did not feel it; I became it. My disappointment quickly turned to anger, which my parents took as being ungrateful. I ran to my room and fell into a deep sadness, without listening to the message of disappointment. I still struggle with wishing for something in my head and wanting that exact object, event or process. I remind myself to S.T.A.R. and listen for the message in the feeling.

The next time you become aware you are feeling disappointed, take a breath and say to yourself, "Keep breathing. I can handle this." Handling disappointment requires letting go of your expectation that things should go a certain way and allowing life to unfold. Seek comfort from a loving source, whether it be a spouse, partner, close friend or God.

Coaching Sad and Its Cousin, Disappointed

Use these words to coach a child who is feeling sad:

Describe: "Your eyes are going like this. Your mouth is going like this."

Name: "You seem sad."

Acknowledge: "I will hold you and be with you. We will get through this together."

Approach and coach a child through disappointment using these DNA words:

Describe: "Your eyes are going like this. Your mouth is going like this."

Name: "You seem disappointed."

Acknowledge: "You were hoping you could spend the night with a friend on a school night. It is hard to wait until the weekend. Breathe with me. You can handle this."

Recognizing Sadness in Yourself and Others

When we feel sad, our eyelids droop as the inner corners of our brows rise and, in extreme sadness, draw together. The corners of our lips pull down, and the lower lip may push up in a pout.

Sad

"Seek comfort from those you love."

Disappointed

"Keep breathing. I can handle this."

The Primary Emotion Happy and Its Cousin, Calm

Everyone wants to be happy, and the benefits are clearly plentiful. Happy people have younger hearts and younger arteries. They recover more quickly from surgery, cope better with pain, have lower blood pressure and have longer life expectancy than unhappy people. Studies also suggest that happy people may have stronger immune systems — they're less likely to get colds and flu viruses. Moreover, when they do, their symptoms tend to be mild. What is this thing called "happiness?" Even scientists, psychologists, theologians and philosophers are unable to define it. Happiness is left for each of us to create our own definition. Some researchers question whether it is even an emotion at all.

In this book, I use "happy" to describe a deep sense of wellbeing and of love. It is not a mere pleasurable feeling, a fleeting emotion or a mood, but an optimal state of being (Ricard, 2007). It is our ever-present natural state of unconditional love that is the essence of who we are. To experience it, we must simply get out of our own way. If we listen to our Emotional Guidance System, it ultimately leads us back to this state of wellbeing. Our EGS reminds us at all times that, while it is impossible to change the world, it is always possible to change the way we perceive it. Happiness is a choice to be who we are: love, loving and loveable. The message of happiness is, "I am love and so are you." It calls us to extend love, to be kind and generous, and to express gratitude.

Emotions are like weather patterns; we cannot stop nor control the weather, we can only respond to it wisely. We often hear the word "calm" in reference to the weather. "We have a calm evening ahead, with no storms on the horizon." You can demonstrate calm (peaceful) to children by shaking up a bottle of water. Notice how the once calm and peaceful water now looks stormy. The shaken water is a great visual for the storm that rages inside us when we are feeling angry or scared. Now, let the water settle into a calm (peaceful) state. This is what our insides look like and feel like when we are feeling calm and peaceful. The message of calm is, "All is well."

When we are able to calm our body and mind, we manufacture predominantly alpha and theta brain waves, signifying that our mind is alert, yet relaxed. This state of relaxed alertness is the optimal learning state. During prolonged periods of relaxation, our body will also secrete protective mood-altering neurotransmitters. One of these, serotonin, is a powerful hormone associated with feelings of happiness and contentment.

Coaching Happiness and Its Cousin, Calm

The next time you are feeling happy, notice your thoughts. Notice how they support this state of happiness. Notice how you are able to see the best in others. Notice how forgiveness and gratitude are so easily accessible.

Notice happiness in a child by using these DNA words:

Describe: "Your eyes are going like this. Your mouth is going like this."

Name: "You seem happy."

Acknowledge: "It is a beautiful day. Wow, just look at all your friends."

Notice calm in a child by using these DNA words:

Describe: "Your eyes are going like this. Your mouth is going like this."

Name: "You seem calm."

Acknowledge: "All is well."

Recognizing Happiness in Yourself and Others

When we feel happy, the corners of the mouth lift in a smile. As the eyelids tighten, the cheeks rise and the outside corners of the brows pull down. Calm is less intense than happy and has a very relaxed facial expression.

Happy
"I am love and so are you."

Calm
"All is well."

Recognizing the emotional world of children provides a powerful voice in their development. Attuning with their emotional states helps children tolerate the distress of uncomfortable emotions long enough to be guided and returned to their primal state of happiness. You cannot simply memorize the DNA dialogues and be an authentic coach for children. If you have ever been on an airplane, you know to put on your oxygen mask before helping someone else. The same is true here: You must first coach yourself before you are ready to coach children. In the next chapter, you will learn the five-step self-regulation process and how to use it with yourself.

Chapter

4

The Adult Journey:
Five Steps for Self-Regulation

We often use the terms "emotion" and "feeling" interchangeably, but there is a difference. Emotions are generated deep within us, beginning on a very unconscious level. We can no more stop an emotion than we can a sneeze. Those of us who can tune into our emotions may feel our chest automatically tighten when anxious or feel our bodies automatically weaken when sad. As I touched on before, emotions are like weather patterns that come and go. We cannot control, manage or change a weather pattern; however, we can accept and embrace it by dressing warmly for a cold front or packing an umbrella for rain. Emotions are similar. We can't control or predict them; however, we can embrace them, allow them to bubble up to conscious awareness and follow the internal guidance they provide.

If we allow an emotion to bubble up naturally through our various brain-body systems, it will eventually rise to a level of consciousness. Once we are aware of it, we can name the emotion and it becomes a feeling. Feelings are conscious and manageable. We can regulate them. The old saying goes, "If you can name it, you can tame it." The key is to allow our unconscious emotions to surface so they can become manageable feelings. As we explored in Chapter 2, if an attuned adult did not respond to particular emotions in our earliest years, we figured out how to distract or distance ourselves from those emotional sensations. We did not learn how to tolerate the discomfort generated in our bodies nor did we learn to trust that emotions are short lived and will soon pass. Instead, we learned to ignore, dismiss, punish, fix, deny and use judgment to project them onto others.

> We cannot coach children in this process until we unlearn the old habits that stymied us and relearn how to become emotionally competent.

The natural process is simple: Something triggers an emotion within us. Left to its own accord, the emotion naturally bubbles up to consciousness where we can manage it as a feeling. Unfortunately, most of us have learned interesting and adaptive ways to keep our emotions out of our awareness. It is critical that we change this dynamic within ourselves and allow our emotions to rise into our conscious awareness so we can regulate and manage them. We cannot coach children in this process until we unlearn the old habits that stymied us and relearn how to become emotionally competent.

The Five-Step Self-Regulation Process

The journey from unconscious emotions to consciously managing our feelings involves five steps: I Am, I Calm, I Feel, I Choose, I Solve. Let's take a quick look at each, and then we will go into greater detail.

Step 1:

 **I Am**

Becoming aware that something has triggered an emotion. A trigger hijacks our present experience and hurls us into our past. Our emotions biochemically overtake us and we become them. "I am angry!"

Step 2:

Breathing deeply and noticing our emotions. We must relax ever so slightly into our emotions rather than reactively judging, distancing, distracting or medicating them. By doing this, we allow our emotions to continue their natural journey into consciousness.

Step 3:

Accurately identifying and naming our emotions. Once we name the emotion, it becomes a conscious feeling we can regulate. Instead of being the emotion, we realize there are two of us, my anger and me. "I feel angry."

Step 4:

Befriending the feeling through acceptance. When we befriend our feelings, we lean into them, relax into the current moment and accept what is instead of what we think should be. In doing so, we open ourselves up to choosing to see from a different perspective in order to move forward. We are empowered to flip the feeling from one of distress to one of calm. From a state of calmness, win-win solutions become apparent.

Step 5:

Awareness is the key to regulation. Steps one through four allow emotions to integrate the mind/brain/body systems into higher awareness. This integrated state allows us to access our internal wisdom, guiding us to the wisest action or decision. Our wisdom always leads us back to a healthier relationship with others and ourselves, and into win-win solutions. Our optimal course may be to see the situation from a different perspective, rewrite a life script, learn new ways to get our needs met or advance our communication skills. The entire process teaches us a new way to handle or perceive the original trigger.

The chart below shows how the lack of emotional awareness and regulation keeps us locked into a perpetual cycle of problems overlaid with addictions, and how the consciously regulated path of the five-step self-regulation process allows continued growth through solutions.

Unconscious	Conscious
I Blame Look what you made me do.	**I Am Triggered** I am angry.
I Demand/Act Out I demand the world go my way. Name calling, etc.	**I Calm** Breathing and noticing nonverbal cues.
I Medicate I medicate the distressing sensations through addiction. Comfort food, etc.	**I Feel** Identify and name the feeling shifting from "I am angry" to "I feel angry."
I Bury I bury my feelings in a life story or life script, painting myself or others as villain or victim, and separating from others.	**I Choose** I relax, change my state and reframe the problem. I can see the situation differently by using positive intent.
I Am Stuck I am stuck in the problem.	**I Solve** Win-win solutions are abundant.

Integrating the Five-Step Self-Regulation Process Into Your Life

Each step of the self-regulation process is discussed at length below, including helpful information and activities.

Step 1: **①** ~~Am~~ / Feel

I Am empowers us to become aware of our emotional triggers. When we first become triggered and experience an emotion, we feel emotionally hijacked. We become our emotions and ready ourselves to act them out in hurtful ways. We are angry. We are frustrated. We are sad. We are afraid. Emotions change how we see the world and how we interpret the actions of others. When we become the emotion, our perception excludes all information that doesn't justify our emotional state. When we are angry, everything we see supports our anger and we ruminate on past injustices. We become the emotion and feel powerless against it. Even our language sets us up to be an uncontrollable mess. We say, "I am so angry!" "I am angry" implies you have no control; you have literally become that emotion. It is your identity. How can we regulate our emotions once we become them? We can't; it's impossible.

The best we can do in this step is to become conscious of and identify our triggers. We have often referred to triggers as things that "push our buttons." Events in our outside world combine with our inner thoughts to stir up our emotions. Many of us are triggered by children who whine, back talk or don't listen when told what to do over and over again. If we do not acknowledge our triggers, we will be perceptually hijacked and treat children the same way we were treated (even though we swore we never would). If whining is a trigger, a whining child approaches you and you unconsciously travel back to your childhood to experience the emotional tone of your upbringing. You open your mouth and out pops something you swore you would never say, usually the words of your own mother or father.

Most triggers are wounds from our past. When activated, these old wounds flood us with a sense of inadequacy, guilt, not being good enough or the need to punish. These sore spots in our souls snatch us away from the present moment, derail our consciousness and set us up for an outburst that will likely hurt others in the same ways we were hurt.

We block all incoming information when we are triggered. We interpret what's happening in a way that fits how we are feeling. Emotions change how we perceive the world and how we interpret the actions of others. We do not challenge if the emotion is inappropriate. We seek to only confirm, defend and justify it (Elkman, 2003). If you are angry, your brain retrieves past experiences and beliefs that support that state. All other information is discarded until this I Am period passes. Ideally, the I Am period lasts only for a second or two, just long enough to focus our attention on the problem at hand. Due to years of overlaying our primary emotions with secondary feelings, however, the I Am stage can last for longer periods of time, perhaps days, weeks, months or even years. This creates huge difficulties in life, biasing the way we see the world and ourselves (and sending divorce rates through the roof).

There are two types of triggers, universal and individual. Universal triggers relate to survival. Someone or something that threatens our lives is a universal trigger for fear. Individual triggers are the ones we create through our unique secondary emotional system. These triggers form a personalized emotional alert database similar to a CD-Rom. When certain life events happen, it's as if they automatically trigger the CD-Rom and we play out the encrypted historical data. Each track on the CD-Rom represents emotional energy that is blocked because of our secondary system. The blocked energy desperately wants to flow freely again. Fortunately, life events show up to give us the opportunity to free this energy by applying the self-regulation process each time we become re-triggered.

Think back to when you were young. Imagine a scene where your parents asked you to do something again and again, to the point of exasperation. See their faces, hear their voices and listen to their words. Now imagine a present-day scene when you have asked a child to do something at least five times. Is your CD-Rom playing a very similar face, voice and phrase?

We all possess CD-Roms full of buttons waiting to be pushed. The good news is that you can rewrite your CD-Rom with the self-regulation techniques we are exploring.

Think of the six distressful feelings below. What would be your unique triggers for each of these feelings? For me, whining can cause an instant reaction of anger. The hairs on the back of my neck stand up, my shoulders tighten and my hands start to burn as anger takes over. A salesperson talking on a cell phone instead of attending to your question, backtalk from a preschooler or traffic may be your anger trigger. Whatever your triggers may be, they bar you from the present moment of attunement and connection. We must become conscious of our triggers if we intend to respond to them differently.

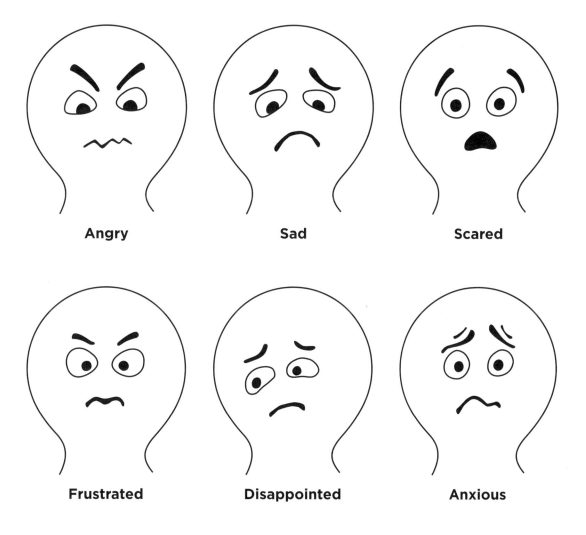

Angry   **Sad**   **Scared**

Frustrated   **Disappointed**   **Anxious**

Activity

This activity will focus on children's behaviors that may be triggers for you. A few sample triggers are already listed to help you begin the process. The following three instructions will guide your process.

1. Check the box beside the prewritten triggers that apply to you.
2. Write additional triggers you currently experience.
3. Take a deep breath, reflect and then write down your top three triggers for each section.

> It may be helpful to complete a similar activity in regard to significant others, family members and coworkers. Keep a journal listing the events where you said or did things you now regret. These events will reveal the patterns to your triggers.

Anger / Frustration Triggers

- ❑ Children who hurt others intentionally. Bullies.
- ❑ Children who don't try or always have an excuse. Lazy.
- ❑ Children who don't listen or care. Apathetic.
- ❑ Children who are disrespectful. Bad attitude.
- ❑ Children who make excuses or blame others. Irresponsible.
- ❑ Children who are arrogant, prejudiced or exclude others. Rude.
- ❑ Children who lack manners and common courtesy. Spoiled.

Additional Triggers for You

- _____

- _____

- _____

Your Top Three Anger/Frustration Triggers

1. _____

2. _____

3. _____

Sadness / Disappointment Triggers

- ❏ When children do not live up to your expectations.
- ❏ Believing the child's parents aren't as caring or loving they should be.
- ❏ Seeing children who are hungry.
- ❏ Believing the child's teachers aren't as caring or professional as they should be.
- ❏ Seeing a child who tries hard but still fails.
- ❏ Hearing school, community or media stories about children with difficult lives.
- ❏ A child who just gives up.
- ❏ Children who lie or bend the truth.
- ❏ Children who say they will do something but don't follow through.

Additional Triggers for You

- _____

- _____

- _____

Your Top Three Sadness/Disappointment Triggers

1. _____

2. _____

3. _____

Scared / Anxious Triggers

❑ A child who does poorly on standardized tests, reflecting poorly on you.

❑ A child who is not learning what he should in the designated time frame.

❑ A parent or teacher has called for an important meeting.

❑ Your supervisor comes to evaluate you or calls you into his or her office.

❑ A child who is aggressive, withdrawn or has other major issues.

❑ Work is due and you are not ready.

❑ A playdate member your child doesn't get along with or two students who are explosive in the same classroom center.

❑ A child hurts another child on your watch and you must tell the parents.

Additional Triggers for You

• _____

• _____

• _____

Your Top Three Scared/Anxious Triggers

1. _____

2. _____

3. _____

Reflection

What I discovered about myself while doing this activity:

_____

_____

_____

Commitment: I am willing to allow myself to become conscious of my emotional triggers. Becoming conscious is not about feeling guilt for past behaviors, it is about changing myself now so I can be more of who I am. I want that for myself, my loved ones and the children in my care.

Signed: _____ Date: _____

As we've said, if we allow them to do so, our emotions will naturally bubble to the surface where we can feel, name and manage them. Scuba diving is one of my favorite hobbies. I like to think of my emotions like the bubbles from my breath rising up through the water to the bright surface above. The bubbles, like my emotions when I allow them, naturally float to the surface. The next step, I Calm, is critical in letting the natural bubbling process occur.

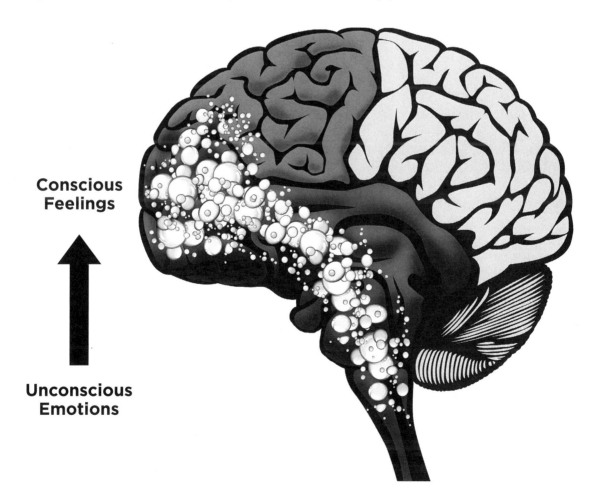

Conscious Feelings

Unconscious Emotions

Step 2: ⓘ Calm

I Calm empowers us to notice and become aware of our emotions. The emotional hijacking that takes place when we become our emotions (I Am) is an instantaneous process. One minute you are walking beside a lake. The next minute you have fallen in, and are flailing around and sinking. We must learn to cut the intensity of this experience in order to manage it. We must get out of the lake before we drown! The only way to accomplish this is to insert a pause between the impulse to act and the action itself. We must breathe!

When we become our emotions, we stress our system and hold our breath. In Conscious Discipline, we teach children and adults a simple active calming technique called S.T.A.R. (**S**mile, **T**ake a deep breath, **A**nd **R**elax). By consciously breathing and focusing our attention on our breath, we are able to turn off the fight or flight stress response of the emotional trigger. Breathing deeply helps to create a pause that empowers us to start to experience rather than become our emotions.

> Creating a pause requires two essential ingredients: Breathing and noticing.

Creating the pause requires not only breathing but also noticing. Noticing asks us simply to see these things as they are, without attaching meaning or judgment. It requires we become the mindful observer. Simply observe the tightness in your chest, the heat in your hands, the rise in your tone of voice or your tendency to move toward the object of your anger. Our culturally conditioned response to these sensations is to judge, not notice. Choosing to notice our inner states instead of judging them asks us to let go of aeons of conditioning. "You stupid jerk," is judgment language for, "My heart is racing and my throat is closing up on me. That car cut me off and scared me half to death!"

A remarkable feature about emotions is their signaling system, as described in Chapter 3. Though we may differ in how expressive we are, emotions have general voice, facial, posture and action signals that broadcast our inner state to others. For example, when we experience sadness, our voice automatically becomes softer and lower, and the inner corners of our eyebrows pull upward

(Ekman, 2003). When we are able to notice the sensations in our body, the signaling expression on our face, our thoughts and our tone of voice when we are triggered, we are on the road to self-regulation.

More often than not, we tend to judge children's behaviors when we feel triggered. Blanketing judgment over children's emotional states inhibits them from accessing their EGS, just as it inhibits us from accessing ours. Judgment, whether perceived as bad or good, blocks the natural flow of emotions from unconscious to conscious awareness.

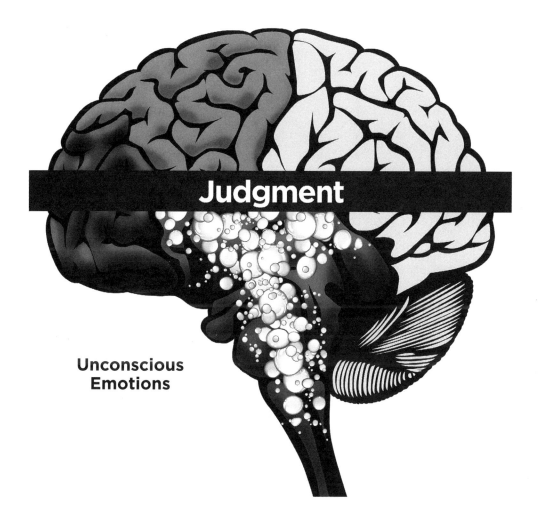

Mindfulness through noticing, instead of judgment, is the key in allowing emotions to become conscious feelings. The following stories of Harley and Cameron will help you further understand the difference.

Harley:

Harley is a four-year-old girl who asked her mother if she could play in the backyard.

Mom curtly says, "No, just stay in the house and play."

"But why can't I?"

Mom feels preoccupied and overwhelmed. "Because I don't want you to. Now be quiet and find something to do. I'm not arguing with you."

Harley puckers her face and begins to cry.

"Stop crying. I said, *no*. Being a crybaby will not change my answer. Go to your room or just go play with something inside."

Mom judges Harley's feelings of disappointment and sadness to be personally irritating, making the situation about her irritation rather than Harley's experience. Mom then overlays Harley's emotional experience with name-calling (crybaby) and abandonment (go to your room).

Cameron:

Cameron is nine years old. He struggles with math and will do anything to avoid it. Today, children are to come to the board and talk through the math problems they did at their desk. Mrs. Trey calls him up to the board. Cameron turns pale, diverts his eyes and slumps low in his seat.

"Cameron, we do not have all day. Get to the board."

He crosses his arms and puts his head down on the desk.

"Cameron get up here now! The problem you have isn't that tough."

Cameron mumbles, "No. I can't."

"Are you going to give up before trying? Is that who you are? A quitter? The whole class is waiting."

Instead of noticing Cameron's fear and anxiousness, Mrs. Trey is judging and overlaying his emotional experience with the message that he is lazy, a quitter and a burden on others.

Over time, these judgments coalesce into beliefs children hold about themselves. They become life themes, scripted stories and perceptions projected onto others. This is exactly how we got the CD-Rom that plays in our heads! Instead, we can choose to breathe and notice, and then facilitate the natural flow of our emotions. In this way, we can stop the cycle of one generation projecting their judgments and past hurts onto the next.

Let's visit the same scenarios and have Mom and Mrs. Trey utilize step two in the self-regulation process. Instead of judging, they will breathe and notice their own triggered state so they can respond differently.

Harley:
Harley asks her mother if she can play in the backyard.

Mother curtly says, "No! You just stay in the house and play." As she hears the tone of her words and feels tightness take over her body, she becomes aware that she is overwhelmed. She willfully attempts to take a few deep breaths and begins noticing the rapid-fire thoughts going through her head: "Can't I have a moment to myself, why does everyone want something from me, why do I have to make all the decisions?" She notices her body is tight all over, notices her eyes feel like disgust is spewing out. She keeps breathing, and then hears her little girl say, "But why can't I?"

"Mommy is working now and you can't go outside by yourself. My job is to keep you safe. Play inside for thirty more minutes, and then I will go out with you. I am going to set the oven timer. When it goes off, we will go outside."

Harley puckers her face and begins to cry.

"It's hard to wait. It's so disappointing! You were hoping we would go outside right now. You can handle this. Breathe with me. We will go out in 30 minutes. What could you do inside to help the time pass quickly?"

Cameron:

Mrs. Trey: "Cameron, we do not have all day. Get to the board." As Mrs. Trey hears her impatient tone of voice, she realizes she is triggered. She immediately attempts a few deep breaths. As she does this, she is able to notice the self-talk in her head: "I have worked with Cameron over and over. He'll never get it. I don't know what else to do. It is not like I don't care but I have 24 other students who need my help. I work hard and can't meet the needs of every student. This is impossible. He just has to try harder." She notices her body is becoming tense and her throat beginning to close up, making it hard to swallow. She continues to breathe and tells the chatter in her head, "I'm safe, keep breathing, I can handle this."

Cameron crosses his arms and puts his head down on the desk.

Mrs. Trey: "Cameron, your arms are going like this. You head is like this."

Cameron peeks out, makes eye contact with his teacher and mumbles, "No. I can't."

Mrs. Trey: "You are choosing to pass. Take your hands and go like this." Mrs. Trey demonstrates the class signal for passing. Cameron does nothing and Mrs. Trey turns to the class and says, "Cameron is having a tough time on this math problem. Let's all take a deep breath and wish him well. He'll get it soon."

Activity

The following activity will help you notice your feelings. In order to make the most of this activity, close your eyes before each section and think about a time when you felt the emotion listed. Generate the story in your mind, as if you were watching a short movie about it. Involve all of your senses in recalling the emotional tone, sensations and internal experience. Then shift your attention from the story (who said/did what to whom) to your body, and begin to notice the internal twitches, tingles, tightness and flutters. Do the following:

1. The first four lines provide model language for noticing instead of judging. Check the ones you have noticed within yourself.
2. The next four lines are left blank for you to write additional thoughts, sensations and actions you notice when you feel that emotion.
3. Beside each section you will also see a blank Buddy. As you complete each section, color the location in the Buddy's body where you notice the emotion. You can color softly, roughly, with different colors, etc., to show the intensity of the sensations you are experiencing.

This example from a participant in the Conscious Discipline Advanced Institute will help guide you:

The story: The most intense sadness I have experienced was for my father's death. I close my eyes and can picture a dozen conversations with him. Conversations, the likes of which I will never experience again... the autumn after college graduation, walking outside crunching acorns beneath our feet as we talk... talking over the dining room table late one night in high school, when the whole house is silent. His eyes and voice are so clear in my mind, it's as if he is still with me, but we can no longer share these quiet conversations together and the sadness of this overwhelms me.

Things I notice about sadness: I let go of the story and focus on the feeling. My throat burns and closes up on me. My eyes turn downward. I feel the heat rising in my face as it tightens up. I want to hide from these difficult sensations. My Buddy drawing shows these sensations.

When I Feel Angry, I Notice...

Replay an anger story in your head. Things I notice about anger:

❑ My face goes like this (demonstrate your face and feel it).

❑ My heart starts to beat fast and I feel an urge to move.

❑ My thoughts turn to all the things people do wrong.

❑ I feel an urge to shop, drink, eat, work, watch TV.

- _____

- _____

- _____

- _____

When I Feel Sad, I Notice...

Replay a sad story in your head. Things I notice about sadness:

❑ My face goes like this (demonstrate and feel it).

❑ My energy level drops. I feel empty and drained.

❑ My thoughts turn to all the things that I have lost.

❑ I feel an urge to shop, drink, eat, work, watch TV.

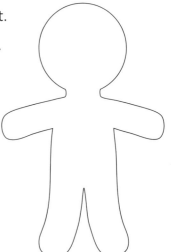

- _____

- _____

- _____

- _____

When I Feel Scared, I Notice...

Replay a scared story in your head. Things I notice about fear:

- ☐ My face goes like this (demonstrate and feel it).
- ☐ My face and body feel frozen. I can't think at all!
- ☐ My fear turns quickly to anxiety.
- ☐ My mind races to, "what if this happens" and "what if that happens."

- _____
- _____
- _____
- _____

When I Feel Happy, I Notice...

Replay a happy story in your head. Things I notice about happiness:

- ☐ My face is going like this (demonstrate and feel it).
- ☐ My body feels strong, centered and energized.
- ☐ My thoughts release judgment and I let things be as they are.
- ☐ I feel an urge to talk, share, be silly and give of myself to others.

- _____
- _____
- _____
- _____

By shifting our attention from the trigger to the breath, we empower ourselves to notice our inner states. We create a tiny pause that short-circuits our desire to judge, project our guilt elsewhere, blame others or act out our emotions, allowing them instead to bubble up to conscious awareness. With practice, we can observe the trigger thoughts flashing through our brains and observe our judgments without saying things we will later regret.

Noticing allows us to learn so much about ourselves! We can see that no one treats us any worse than we treat ourselves. We can see we still carry around a lot of anger, sadness and fear from the times when we allowed ourselves to become our emotions; times when, instead of getting out of the lake, we tried to pretend, distract or deny we were in it. We can see that we're blocking our happiness in a big way, and that the pause we've created in this step will empower us to name, befriend, regulate and learn from our feelings instead of being a victim to life events.

Step 3: **❶Feel**

I Feel empowers us to name our feelings. As this emotion (energy in motion) continues its journey to awareness, the next step is to put a name on all the sensations we are experiencing. Emotions are energetic, physiological constructs consisting of thoughts, beliefs and feelings. We must pull the feeling out of the conglomerate. In order to do this, we must be willing to let go of the story and name the primary feeling represented by the story.

This simple naming process creates a shift that separates us from the emotion. Instead of "I am angry," losing my identity in an out-of-control state, we shift to "I feel angry." When we drop the stories and name the feelings, we create space, a little distance that allows us to feel our feelings instead of become them.

We automatically create space when we name the feeling, however, naming is not as simple as it sounds. Most of us simply haven't had much help or practice with this skill! We often block the process by doing one of four things:

Block #1: Burying the feeling by believing the story. Remember, when we are triggered and in the "I am my emotions" state, we block all incoming information that does not support our current emotional state. We create a perception in those moments, a story about how we were victimized in some way and collect all possible data to support it. Creating a story from limited understanding and perceptual abilities (while in the lake) encapsulates our emotions and protects them from change. How many of us carry around stories and emotional baggage from our childhood? Essentially, we trust the perception of a nine-year-old child to guide our current lives and interactions.

Block #2: Confusing a thought with a feeling. We confuse a thought with a feeling by saying, "I feel like _____," or, "I feel as if _____," instead of saying, "I feel _____," followed by a feeling word. "I feel like you are not listening" is a thought, not a feeling. "I feel as if you're just trying to sway my vote" is a thought, not a feeling. "I feel frustrated" is a feeling. Since naming our feelings is new for many of us, start with using the basic core feelings: angry, scared, sad and happy. When you feel emotionally triggered, pick one of these four feelings and give the bodily sensations a name.

Block# 3: "I feel upset" or "I feel fine." We often lump feelings into general categories: "I feel upset" or "I feel fine." These generalizations block the embedded feeling message from coming into our awareness. Think of trying to get a message to Jason in a classroom full of children by calling out, "Children, children," instead of "Jason, Jason." You might never hear from "Jason" because you called out the blanket descriptor, "children."

The categories of "upset" and "fine" are the same as "pleasant" and "unpleasant." As I mentioned in the introduction, these are the same categories we began life with as infants. We have grown cognitively and physically, yet our emotional development is stymied at the level of a two-year-old child. Most of us probably need to pause to accurately identify the core feelings of anger, sadness, happiness and fear. Identifying the cousin feelings (frustrated, anxious, disappointed and calm) can be even more difficult. However, accurately naming our feelings is key to freeing ourselves up to feel them, and ultimately to regulate and listen to them.

Block# 4: Using the language of judgment. We use the language of judgments like sarcasm, criticism and silence instead of the language of feelings. The language of feelings brings us closer together, building a bridge from the problem to the solution, from rejection to connection. Criticism, sarcasm and silence create roadblocks to communication and connection. Without connection, we are cut off from the higher centers of the brain and once again thwart our attempts at self-control, goal achievement and relationship success.

Shifting from the language of judgment to the language of feelings requires a pause. This cannot happen if we allow ourselves to remain on unconscious autopilot. The list below contains judgment statements and their corresponding feeling statements. Notice how discovering the feeling words changes the intent of the communication from judging (attacking) to sharing (connecting).

Judgment	Feeling
You are just trying to make this hard!	I feel anxious that we are having trouble.
Look at world politics. We are going to blow each other up!	I feel sacred. I don't know how to make a political difference.
You don't care about me.	I feel disappointed. I was hoping we could have more time together.
Are your legs broken? Look at all that still needs to be done before the party!	I feel overwhelmed. How about giving me a hand with the party stuff? You can set up the drinks and ice.
You keep lying to me!	I feel confused. Please help me understand.

You might think it's a lot of work to change your emotional speech. It is, and it requires vigilance and consciousness. However, this small shift in attention is the difference between, "I'm going to blow your head off!" and "I feel furious." It is the difference between perpetual conflict and world peace. Commit to yourself today that as soon as you feel yourself becoming emotional, you will take a deep breath and find the feeling word. Give that emotion a name so you can begin the process of self-regulation and peace.

For years, I have struggled with my own anger issues. When I finally learned to feel anger instead of become it, I was able to manage it better. Read the following lines slowly. See if you can feel a difference within your body.

> I am angry.   I feel angry.
> I am sad.   I feel sad.

Could you feel a difference? My body seemed a little more relaxed when I say, "I feel" rather than "I am." Returning to the metaphor of the lake, "I am angry," is akin to jumping into a lake without knowing how to swim. We flail around, fight the process and often strike out at those who try to help us. When we say, "I feel angry," we suddenly become a person who is experiencing a particular feeling and has the power to control it. Instead of jumping into the lake of the emotion, we can choose to sit beside the lake, feel the feeling and listen quietly and patiently for the message and guidance it offers.

The simple shift from "You are angry" to "You seem (or sound) angry" is powerful. It encourages children to look within and name the emotion they are experiencing. The sooner they become aware of the emotion, the better their odds of putting a tiny pause between feeling the emotion and the impulsive action it might elicit. That tiny pause is the difference between hitting someone back or saying, "I don't like it when you hit me. When you want to play say, *Will you play with me?*"

Step 4: **❶ Choose**

I Choose empowers us to befriend our feelings. Naming a feeling provides the opportunity to tame it and the choice to reframe it. Befriending and embracing the feeling empowers us to act consciously within the realm of choice. The opportunity to choose different outcomes happens with the naming process, but the action itself requires we befriend the feeling we have named. Befriending our feelings can be difficult. Sometimes we fear letting a feeling in; it may act like an oh-too-happy houseguest and never leave. Other times, we may fear our feelings will rule the roost. When we allow ourselves to be aware of a feeling, we often attempt to keep it quietly off in the distance. In actuality, befriending our feelings is the only thing that allows them to move on.

> What we resist persists. What we accept evaporates.

How do we befriend a feeling? Think of how you develop friendships. The first step is to say, "Hello," offering a simple acknowledgement. The next step is some form of invitation, "Would you like to join me for a chat?" The underlying message to the emotion is, "Welcome. It's okay for you to be here, you are safe. I will not condemn you, push you away, deny you, medicate you or stifle you any longer."

As we learn to welcome our feelings, lean into them and embrace their presence, we allow them to do their job of integration. They integrate our autonomic nervous system, balancing the parasympathetic (pause) and sympathetic (speed up). They integrate our personality by embracing lost parts of ourselves. They integrate our physiology, promoting optimal physical health. They integrate our lower brain systems with our higher brain systems, allowing us to respond instead of react to life events. They encourage us to stop resisting what is and demanding the world go our way, and empower us to move through life with grace and acceptance. In short, they allow us to adapt to what life offers instead of fight it.

Befriending our feelings gives us the opportunity to make a choice, to see things differently. When we are gripped by an emotion, our perception is narrowed significantly in order to support that emotion. Now we can choose to see a problem from many sides. We are free to rewrite any past story by using positive intent thus creating a happy ending for others and ourselves.

In reference to my story in Chapter 2 about "my dad is killing my mom," once I pulled out the feelings of anger and fear, I was guided to a new perception. I could feel my anger of being unable to stop the devastating disease that was slowly robbing my parents of their minds. I could feel my fear of being parent-less, and the fear of how I might someday have the same devastating disease. As I accepted these emotions and allowed them to be with me, I started to see the love story between my mom and dad. My dad loved my mother, stood by her, and nurtured her throughout the disease.

I also remember the day I discovered my "can't ever measure up" life story. I wrote this script for myself as I competed with my brother for parental favor. One day it dawned on me that this perceptual lens was created in the mind of a jealous three-year-old Becky. I have been around many three-year-olds and never would I turn my life over to their reasoning skills. Yet, that is what I had done for almost five decades!

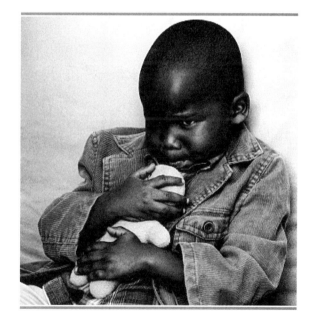

Life themes such as "trust no one," "being right equals being safe," or "pleasing others equals love" are just as silly. Whatever your story is, only the feeling is true. Name the feeling, befriend it and get busy rewriting!

Think of something in your life you find fearful at this moment. "Scared" might not be the word you would choose, so consider the many cousins of scared (concerned, worried, anxious). Imagine holding the feeling safely in your arms, keeping it in your back pocket or putting it in your purse as you go about your day. Simply allowing the feeling to be with you until its integrative work is done is a gift.

Step 5: 🄸 Solve

I Solve empowers us to take action based on the wisdom of our feelings. We have identified our triggers, learned to calm our emotions through breathing and noticing, named our feelings and returned to our natural state of wholeness by befriending them. Now we can use the message within the feelings and the brilliance generated from their integration to take action. We do this by communicating from a position of responsibility. "Responsibility" means "I am responsible for my feelings, I am responsible for my thoughts and I am responsible for my actions." Responsible adult solutions include conflict resolution, acceptance, learning a new skill and building stronger connections. True solutions always create a win-win stuation. In Chapter 3 we discussed feeling messages. The feeling messages below point you toward responsible, win-win solutions:

Anger and frustration are motivating energies that deliver the message of change. Do I want others to change how they treat me? Do I want things to happen differently? Do I want to achieve certain goals? Do I want to rewrite a life story? Anger and frustration ask you to clearly define what you *want* instead of what you *don't want*. To do this, you must first calm yourself and turn off the fight or flight response in your body. The antidote to anger is breathing and calming.

Examples of how to respectfully share anger:

- "I feel angry. I am going to calm myself and then I'll talk with you."
- "I don't like it when you talk when I am talking. Please wait until I have finished my sentence."
- "I feel frustrated. I was hoping we could talk this through calmly."

Sadness and disappointment carry the message of loss. How do I handle losing opportunities or losing someone dear to me? Sadness and disappointment ask us to seek comfort, help and understanding, and to be conscious that what we are seeking will provide comfort. Just recently, my father passed away. It took me almost a week to consciously become aware that I was seeking comfort from cookies while staring at one television show after another rather than seeking the comfort of those who love me. Many of us have life themes that prevent us from seeking help. Many of us mistakenly believe that asking for help is a sign of weakness, meaning we are vulnerable. We associate vulnerability with painful experiences. Many of us believe that when we allow ourselves to be vulnerable, we open ourselves up to additional disappointment or sadness if the response we hope for is not forthcoming. The antidote to these feelings is to seek comfort from love and to have faith.

Examples of dialogues for sharing sadness and disappointment include:

- "I feel disappointed. I was hoping we would go out to dinner tonight. Would you help me get some sandwiches for the kids and tell me I can handle tonight, no matter how it turns out?"
- "I feel sad. I miss my mom. I know she passed years ago, but it seems that waves of sadness still rush over me. Would you just hold me?"

Scared and anxious carry the message of threat, whether it is real or imagined. Scared and anxious are a call for safety. Because many of us experienced a great deal of threat growing up, we don't even know what real safety feels like or looks like. As a result, we underestimate how intimidating we are to others as we act out our fear instead of communicating it. Safety comes from reassurance, obtaining more information, seeking shelter, or having someone or something physically protecting us from harm. The antidote to fear is safety.

Examples of how to share the feelings of scared and anxious:

- "I feel anxious about work deadlines. I don't know if I can meet them. I was hoping for more time and more information about the exact nature of the task."
- "I feel scared. This car is not safe. I am going to rent a car until our car is fixed and I feel it is safe to drive."

Happy and calm hold the overall message that many of us strive to achieve: Life is good. Yet, happy and calm are not something you achieve or work at, they are the state we relax into when we stop resisting "what is." Happy and calm is our natural state. Babies and young children live in a natural state of happy and calm, of joy! The message of happy and calm is to remember to be grateful, to remember love is the answer regardless of the problem and to remember we are all connected.

This final step, I Solve, will lead us back to our original trigger with new insight and skills. In my story with my mom and dad, I was empowered to approach my trigger, "Dad is going to kill Mom," with a new perspective of their impressive and hard-fought love story. As we repeat this five-step process over and over again, we heal ourselves, improve our relationships and make choices that move us closer to achieving our goals.

At this point, you might be ready to make a change in your life. I've cited research, discussed strategies and explored enough examples to sufficiently pave the way. The five steps of self-regulation do not come automatically; we must practice them ourselves, consciously and with vigilance. The more we are willing to change ourselves and improve our self-regulation skills, the better we can coach and interact with our children and with each other. What we offer to others we strengthen in ourselves. See the best and you become your best, guaranteed!

Now it's time to apply all we've learned toward helping children. As parents and educators, we tend to want to leave the world a bit better than it was when we arrived. We want each generation to be a bit wiser, happier and more fullfilled than ours. The next chapter contains information that is vital to helping us manifest this passion.

Commitment: I am willing to practice the five-step self-regulation process with myself. I now realize that asking a child to do something I am not willing to do myself sets us both up for failure.

Signed: _____ Date: _____

Chapter 5

The Child's Journey:
Coaching Children in the Five-Step Process

"I had it first." "I hate you." "This is stupid." "You can't make me." "No, no, no!" Children's emotional outbursts encompass a variety of outward behaviors from pushing and shoving to name-calling and exclusion. They also are expressed inwardly through withdrawal, perfectionism and sulking. How we respond to children's emotions will either inhibit or encourage the emergence of their self-regulatory skills.

Helping children to manage their feelings and coaching them from unconsciously *reacting* to their emotions to consciously *responding* to them requires the same five-step process adults experience. The understanding you have gained about your Emotional Guidance System (EGS) and the five-step self-regulation process will provide you with great insight toward coaching children through the same process.

When teaching children the self-regulation process, you must provide them with something to refer to and hold. It is helpful to use the set of eight Buddies that come with the *Feeling Buddies Self-Regulation Toolkits* mentioned in the Introduction. If you do not choose to purchase a *Feeling Buddies Toolkit*, download the *"How Do You Feel"* chart from the Conscious Discipline website. Print, cut out, laminate and Velcro the feeling faces from this chart onto dolls or stuffed animals you already have to make emotional recognition dolls as a substitute for the Feeling Buddies.

A very basic explanation of the process is that the child selects the Feeling Buddy that corresponds to how she is feeling based on the expression on the Buddy's face. The adult then coaches her to apply the five-step self-regulation process to the Feeling Buddy. As she learns to apply the five steps of self-regulation to her Feeling Buddy, she is also practicing how to conduct the process with herself. This draws on the principle stated in Chapter 1: "What you offer to others, you strengthen within yourself."

Before we look at the child's steps in-depth, take a moment to reflect upon the following summaries. As you read, allow your mind to see the similarities between the five steps in the adult's self-regulation process and the child's journey.

Step 1:

Triggered. The child, like the adult, is triggered by an event or interaction. At this moment emotions flood the child who filters all incoming information to support the emotion he is experiencing. Every parent and teacher has experienced these moments with young children. There could be fifteen red markers on the table, but Jacob wants *that one*. Nothing will persuade him to let go of wanting *that one*. He will stick to his story, collect data to support his desire, will not let go and may even lie or throw a tantrum, all in an effort to get the world to go his way. His focus narrows and he excludes all additional incoming information. This triggered period may be as brief as a few seconds or could last hours. To help a child progress to step two, we must remain calm in the moment of upset and help the child begin to calm.

Ultimately, we must also get to know children well enough to identify their triggers and the ways they attempt to self-calm so we can help them do the same for themselves. Once the child is aware of his triggers, he will be able to choose to go to the Safe Place to begin his own self-regulatory process (with additional coaching and assistance). The Safe Place is a structure for the home or classroom that provides children with the opportunity to practice the five-step self-regulation process with themselves and their Feeling Buddies.

Step 2:

🄸 Calm

Breathe and notice. The goal in step two is to help the child create a momentary pause between becoming lost in her emotion (I Am) and acting out. When we become our emotions, we react from the unconscious lower centers of our brain. Creating a pause makes a more conscious response possible. To help the child create a pause, we encourage her to take three deep breaths. This deep belly breathing helps shut off the fight or flight response in the body. We then notice and describe the child's nonverbal emotional signals. Noticing brings the child's awareness to her body, thus beginning the process of separating her identity from the emotion. Noticing also promotes eye contact, which fosters connection. Connection enables us to use mirror neurons to facilitate the active calming process through downloading.

Step 3:

Naming the feeling. Many children can identify feelings in a picture, but have a difficult time identifying what they are feeling while they are upset. Our job in this step is to coach children to discover their feelings while in an upset state. This helps the child separate the feeling from his identify. This journey from "I *am* angry" to "I *feel* angry" is the essential step that allows for self-regulation to occur.

If you are in the Safe Place with the child, you will encourage her to select the Feeling Buddy or the substitute emotional recognition doll that best shows how she is feeling. If you are in the middle of a teachable moment where the child is acting out her emotions through talking back, name calling or other forms of disrespectful communication, you will offer the child your best educated guess about what she is feeling by sharing the emotion first and the behavior second using the DNA process (as explained in Chapter 3). Simply saying, "Your face is going like this. You seem angry. You wanted _____," at the appropriate time makes a world of difference. When we help the child accurately name the emotion, the feeling becomes manageable and the integration process can begin in earnest.

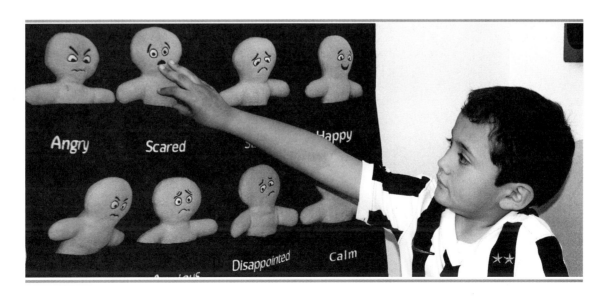

Step 4:

Accept and reframe. In this step, we will help the child accept and befriend the feeling in order to change it. With acceptance, the integrative process naturally provides the child with the willingness to change the feeling state and learn from the original trigger. Changing a feeling state from upset to calm is essential for rejoining the class or family in a healthy, respectful way. Our job is to assist children in making healthy choices for shifting and returning to their optimal state. In addition to the four core strategies of S.T.A.R., drain, balloon and pretzel, other choices that will help the child shift include the Story Hand, journal writing, drawing and talking. The child will often hold onto his Buddy or emotional recognition doll as he progresses.

Step 5:

Solutions. You did it! You coached the child through the first four self-regulatory steps necessary to create a pause between impulse and action. Now that the child is in an optimal learning state, we can teach a new skill or a new perception to the original trigger. Our job in step five is to coach the child to handle the trigger differently in order to solve the problem the next time it occurs. We will prompt and encourage solutions that may involve environmental changes or new social skills. The five categories of solutions we will facilitate are:

1. Conflict resolution.
2. Accepting and responding to your feelings.
3. Learning a new skill.
4. Structuring the environment visually for success.
5. Establishing stronger connections.

> Establishing a firm working knowledge of the five steps detailed in this chapter is the key to success when helping children learn to regulate their emotions well enough to solve problems in respectful, healthy ways.

Coaching Methods

There are three different coaching methods that will help adults and children become proficient at regulating their thoughts, feelings and actions:

1. Daily **teachable moments**.
2. The **Safe Place** self-regulation learning center.
3. The songs and activities in the ***Feeling Buddies Curriculum***.

This book provides information for coaching self-regulation in teachable moments and in the Safe Place. These two coaching methods are basically the same for both parents and teachers. The songs and activities in the *Feeling Buddies Curriculum* are specific to educators, and are provided in the *Feeling Buddies Self-Regulation Toolkit for Teachers* available from ConsciousDiscipline.com. A Curriculum sample can be found at the end of this book.

Teachable Moments

Teachable moments occur throughout the day as children and adults experience emotional distress. Most of us call these moments of conflict "discipline events." Just remember, all conflict starts with emotional upset. Real discipline and guidance are impossible unless we can manage the upset first. During teachable moments, the adults must self-regulate in order to successfully implement the five steps.

The benefit of using teachable moments is that they make a beeline to imprinting new skills. Brain research and common sense tells us that in order to learn new skills for managing an emotional state, we must put them into use when the emotional state is activated. Everyone has used words and tactics in the heat of the moment that they later regret. We also know that if we had been able to manage our emotions better, we could have handled the situation better. What if, in these heated moments, we became coaches for children to help them manage their emotions and wire their brains for self-regulation? Teachable moments provide a wonderful opportunity to do just that. When the child becomes triggered, the adult self-calms and then assists the child in conducting her own five-step self-regulation process.

The Safe Place

The Safe Place is a sacred space where children are instructed, encouraged and supported in attending to their own emotional upsets through self-regulating activities. It is the learning center where children apply the self-regulation skills we have taught them during teachable moments. It is a place where they are safe to practice these new skills with themselves and with their Feeling Buddies or other emotional recognition dolls.

> Help children recognize "I am triggered" and take themselves to the Safe Place.

Children go to the Safe Place to change their inner state from upset to calm. They are free to use it as needed, and can use it as long as is needed. I use the word "sacred" in describing the Safe Place to signify the trust and respect required from the adult for the Safe Place to successfully fulfill its function for children (Bailey, 2011). The Safe Place is not "Time Out" where children are sent to their room or removed from the classroom activities. It is a learning center similar in concept to the science center at school where students learn about magnets, or the kitchen at home where children learn about cooking.

The Safe Place consists of the following:

- A comfortable **physical structure** to sit on or in (beanbag, chair, soft pillows).

- A visual display of the **I Calm active calming icons**. Children need visual prompts that support each step of the self-regulatory process. Visual icons for S.T.A.R., drain, balloon and pretzel can be downloaded at no cost from the Conscious Discipline website. The *I Calm Safe Place Mat* provides the icons in a multi-sensory form and can be purchased at ConsciousDiscipline.com.

- Whether you purchased a ***Feeling Buddies Toolkit*** or have created your own emotional recognition dolls using the images on ConsciousDiscipline.com, introduce them to the children and keep them in the Safe Place. This allows children to interact with them independently. As children help their Buddies learn to self-regulate, they also help themselves do the same.

- ***I Choose: Self-Control Board*** provides individualized choices to help children learn how to regulate their emotions and learn how to change them. The activities on the *I Choose Board* include I Love You Ritual connection activities, the four core calming strategies and reflective activities such as journal writing. The *I Choose Board* is available for purchase at ConsciousDiscipline.com.

- Fill your Safe Place with **class or homemade books** and commercial children's literature that support the five-step self-regulation process. The *Shubert* book series, which is part of the Conscious Discipline program, provides excellent support for your Safe Place. They are available for purchase on ConsciousDiscipline.com. *Shubert is a S.T.A.R.* introduces the calming strategies and the Safe Place in the story.

- Provide **visuals**. The right hemisphere of the brain, where self-regulation is controlled, loves pictures and images. It is therefore essential to post visual representations of the five-step process (I Am, I Calm, I Feel,

I Choose and I Solve). You will also want to post pictures of children conducting the five-step process. For example, an *I Calm* picture might include a child demonstrating the Pretzel. Several of these visuals can be downloaded from ConsciousDiscipline.com.

You can see the Safe Place in action by visiting Shubert's Classroom and watching the videos provided on ConsciousDiscipline.com. You can also learn more about the Safe Place by reading *Conscious Discipline: the Seven Basic Skills for Classroom Management* (Bailey, 2000) and *Creating the School Family: Bully-Proofing Classrooms Through Emotional Intelligence* (Bailey, 2011).

The Five-Step Process

Now let's explore each of the five steps in greater depth, utilizing common child-centric examples to clarify what each step might look like in practice. You will see some steps subdivided by coaching model (Safe Place, Teachable Moments) where it is helpful to do so. All five steps are presented in linear form; however, they are fluid and circular when applied in real life. The more you practice the process, the more natural it will become.

Step 1: **ⓘ Am**

Triggered. By now we are well acquainted with what "becoming our emotions" entails. Our immediate response to the child at this "I Am" stage of emotional arousal can worsen or help heal the upset. Helping children with their triggers involves the following four actions from adults:

1. Be willing and vigilant about regulating ourselves.
2. Observe and learn the universal triggers and the particular triggers for an individual child or group.
3. Observe children carefully to see how they attempt to calm themselves when triggered. Some children may run, some hide under the sink, some play with their hair and some collapse quickly into tantrums.
4. Teach children to become aware of their own triggers and go to the Safe Place to self-regulate.

Children who are over-reactive have "I Am" periods that come on quickly and last a long time. Imagine those moments in your own life when you are so stressed that a sock left on the living room floor puts you completely over the edge. Some children are so stressed that they live in this highly aroused state. They have little ability to deal with the added discomfort of their emotions and explode easily. These children require additional care and diligence from us. Above all else, we must remember to breathe and remain calm so we can help these volatile children work through their triggers and the self-regulatory steps they so desperately require.

Twelve toddlers in the same room at a daycare is, in essence, a trigger. It's just a matter of time before one steps on the other, grabs a toy or becomes over-whelmed with the noise. Our job is to get to know our children well enough to see the world from their point of view. I was born with mild to moderate sensory issues. Tags in my shirts throw me into fits of craziness. I would rather die than walk barefoot in mud. As a child, anything scratchy on my skin could lead to a meltdown, which is why I refused to take ballet and wear an "itchy tutu." Growing up, I was very vocal about my distress, so these things were not a secret. Yet my mother never seemed to understand. She would buy lacy outfits and fuss at me for complaining about the scratchiness. I would only wear certain clothes, mostly soft cotton. Mom would go crazy about the laundry issues I was creating when there were plenty of clean clothes in the closet but I would wear the same ones over and over. She could never see the world from my point of view. She kept insisting things should be different, and by default that I should be different, too.

Getting to know children well enough to understand their triggers requires letting go of what *should be* and what *doesn't make sense* to us, and to start *observing* our children. We must suspend judgment long enough to see from the child's point of view. Pay attention to how the child reacts to your response to his triggered reaction. Notice the child's body, nonverbal cues and verbal ones. If the child's body begins to relax, eyes soften and his voice begins to return to normal, your response to him has been helpful. If the child's body becomes tight, his face hardens and his tone becomes harsh, then you know your response was not helpful.

I know adults who insist on "helping" their teenage children by giving lectures and offering crystal ball predictions. ("If you keep this up you'll never get into college.") If they would simply observe their teens, they would see their "help-fulness" was actually throwing the teens deeper into a fight or flight survival state. They would notice the teens withdrawing or lashing out. An outside observer can often see these triggers; however, parents sometimes become too involved to see them themselves. We must be in the higher centers of our brain to observe someone's behaviors. From a triggered state, we can only see our own judgments and bias.

Ari is a young boy who has a great deal of trouble managing his impulses. Lety Valero, the co-creator of the *Feeling Buddies Curriculum*, is the principal of Eton School where Ari attends. She noticed Ari naturally trying to calm his anger by going to the computer. She also learned from Ari's mother that he watches a lot of television in an attempt to calm his overwhelmed nervous system at home. Mrs. Valero's approach to Ari was to help him create a movie he could watch in the Safe Place. In the movie, Ari talks to himself and demonstrates the steps he needs to take to self-regulate. On the *Feeling Buddies DVD* that is included in the *Feeling Buddies Self-Regulation Toolkits*, you can see the movie Ari and Mrs. Valero created. Now when Ari comes to the Safe Place, he watches his movie to coach himself through the steps that will help him successfully manage his anger. Children are constantly sending us messages and signaling what could be helpful. We must be calm enough and conscious enough to hear them.

Elizabeth Montero-Cefalo, one of our Loving Guidance Associates, was observing a young boy with autism to see what he tended to do when he became overwhelmed. This particular boy would go to the sink to turn the water on and off. This prompted Mrs. Montero-Cefalo to provide a wave bottle in the Safe Place to help him learn how to regulate himself in a socially acceptable manner. The child would take himself to the Safe Place and use the wave bottle as his first step in calming his over-aroused nervous system. Another child with autism entered the program. She offered him the same wave bottle to calm down, and he threw it across the room. Each child soothes in a different way.

We must observe each child individually. Each child will also experience unique triggers; however, some triggers are universal. The list below offers insight on several universal triggers for young children.

Nutritional and Energy Triggers: A child who is hungry, thirsty, bloated, experiencing intestinal distress, tired, hyped up on sugar or sleepy is more likely to be easily triggered.

Attachment Triggers: Every child needs a trusting, attuned relationship with the adults that care for and teach her. Genetically, children are programmed to seek out this attachment figure for safety and survival during times of distress. A young child without this crucial bond at school will become triggered during typical bonding activities such as naptime, eating, diapering and toileting.

Punishment and Trauma Triggers: Children who received harsh punishments or experienced trauma will be triggered by similar events. If a child has been hit repeatedly, the simple motion of the child next to him raising her hand could trigger explosive emotions.

Aggressive and Intrusion Triggers: Victims of aggressive behaviors often become triggered. This occurs whether the aggression is physical (hitting or grabbing), verbal (name-calling) or social (you can't play with us).

Unpredictability Triggers: Children need a predictable and consistent environment for optimal development of their arousal system. The brain seeks out patterns. When we detect a pattern, our systems relax. When we cannot identify the pattern, our systems stay on high alert. Lack of visual predictability can be a trigger for many children.

Approval and Validation Triggers: Children seek relationships with adults for survival. Adults often exploit the child's natural willingness to please by manipulating it as a discipline strategy. Statements like, "I like the way Ryan is sitting," exemplify this subtle manipulation. For some children, feeling they have disappointed an adult can be a trigger. Children also seek validation of what they are experiencing. Telling some children what to think or feel can be a trigger. ("She's your friend. You know you don't hate her. Give her a hug.")

Belonging Triggers: We want to feel that we make a difference in the world, that we belong to something greater than ourselves, that we can be of service and that we are helpful people. Removing children harshly ("Just go to your room,"), creating competitive classrooms ("The first table ready will…"), using external rewards ("If you're good, you will receive…") and relying on abandonment strategies ("If you aren't ready by the time I count to three, we are leaving you here,") can all be triggers.

Failure Triggers: As children mature, they move from dependence to a more independent skill set. They want to do things for themselves and for others. The inability to get the car door open alone, finish a puzzle or draw a picture can be a trigger.

Sensory Triggers: Many children with or without documented sensory integration dysfunction (SID) have sensory triggers. The noise in the classroom, light quality, food textures, touch or overwhelming visuals can be triggers. In my case, the clothes I wear can over-arouse my system. Specially trained occupational and/or physical therapists can assist you with these issues (Kranowitz, 1998).

Motor Control Triggers: For some children, sitting on the floor crisscross applesauce requires all their attention and effort, leaving no ability to "learn" at circle time. Physical and/or occupational therapists can help with these triggers.

Language Triggers: Most young children do not have the language skills to deal with all that happens in group settings like playdates and childcare. We must coach them in social and communication skills so they can set successful limits with their friends and get their needs met in a socially acceptable manner. In addition, some children may have speech and language development issues that require careful observation and adaptations to be successful. Speech therapists can help with these triggers.

Environmental Demand Triggers: Removing play and social-emotional components from the early childhood classrooms in the name of teaching academic readiness is putting tremendous stress on children and teachers. This early academic curriculum is a trigger for many children. In addition, parents often believe their children must play structured sports to get ahead. Structured learning that lacks sufficient playtime at too young an age creates enormous amounts of stress and potential triggers for young children.

Take a moment to think about a child who has a hard time managing his emotions. These children are labeled "discipline problems" at school and "difficult" children at home because they act out emotional states instead of managing them. Now think about things that trigger the child's anger, sadness or fear. Remember, acting out can look like hitting, pushing, name-calling and throwing objects. Make a list below:

Child	Trigger	Emotion Generated
1.		
2.		
3.		

If you could not come up with two triggers, commit to observing the child more closely. Release your judgment, manage your own emotions and just notice him or her throughout the day. What triggers the child and what does the child tend to do to manage those triggers (hide, yell, hit, cry, etc.)?

Knowing a child's triggers allows the adult to increase a child's success by doing one or more of the following:

1. **Change the environment so the child is more successful.**
    *   At school, seat a child who struggles with regulation directly across from you at circle time and seat an assistant beside her. At home, seat this child across from you at mealtimes and when helping him with his homework. Sitting across from each other provides you with the best view of all the child's nonverbal and verbal signals. *We often tend to put these children beside us so we can "control" them instead of observe and guide them.*

- Partner a child who struggles with attention and regulation issues with a child who can be a mentor and model for these behaviors. *Often we remove children by placing them in time out (home) or removing them from the classroom (school).*

- Provide clear visual images of expected behaviors in a variety of contexts. *We often rely on verbal commands, threats and prompts. Self-regulation is a right hemisphere job and requires images for the children to be successful.*

- Provide clear boundaries delineating personal space. At school, teachers often provide a carpet square, chair or even a laundry basket to help children know what space is theirs. At home, parents will need to provide specific seats at mealtimes, placemats and other clear spatial boundaries instead of constantly demanding siblings share. *Often, instead of structuring the environment for children to be successful, we allow them to do as they please as long as they do not disrupt others.*

- Offer opportunities for food at different times of the day. *We often demand children eat on our schedule, regardless of their life experiences and whether or not they are hungry.*

- At school, vary the class schedule to allow for different group sizes, brain breaks, relaxing times and activities requiring different degrees of attention. At home, provide children with indoor and outdoor time, and a break after school and before homework time. *Often, we demand children pay attention without structuring the day with the brain in mind.*

2. **Change your response patterns to the child's behavior.**
   - Notice carefully if your response to the child's behavior is worsening (escalating) or improving it (de-escalating).
   - Remember to employ active calming strategies and to be a S.T.A.R. (**S**mile, **T**ake a deep breath, **A**nd **R**elax) to move from unconscious reactions to attuned responses.
   - Access your own brilliance and use the five steps in this book.

3. **Teach the child a socially acceptable way of meeting his/her needs.**
   - Instead of trying to stop the behaviors you don't want ("Our rule is no hitting,"), transform behaviors ("When you want a turn, tap

him on his shoulder, hold out your hand and say, *May I have a turn please?*").

4. **Help the child handle situations that are out of his or her control with compassion, calming strategies and problem-solving**.
   - *"This is difficult. You were hoping your friend would be at your school with you forever. It's hard when a friend moves to another school. Keep breathing. You can handle this. We'll find ways for you to write her notes and talk to her as soon as she is settled with a new address."*

5. **Assist, coach and encourage children to go to the Safe Place to learn and practice self-regulation.**

Step 2: ① Calm

Breathe and notice. The three skills of active calming, noticing and downloading are necessary for adults to help children become aware of and manage their emotions. These skills are integral to the Conscious Discipline program (Bailey 2000, 2011) and the five step process. These skills allow the unconscious emotions to continue bubbling up from the lower centers of the brain to the higher centers where choice, learning and adaptability are possible.

Active Calming Strategies for Children

Active calming techniques disengage the stress response. You must teach these active calming strategies to children when they are calm so they can access them or be coached when in an upset state. The following four core Conscious Discipline techniques are essential:

S.T.A.R.: S.T.A.R. is an acronym for **S**mile, **T**ake a deep breath, **A**nd **R**elax. Taking three deep breaths turns off the fight or flight response in the body. The simple act of attempting to smile when triggered begins changing our inner states. Sometimes for children we will also use **S**top, **T**ake a deep breath, **A**nd **R**elax in teaching moments.

Drain: Extend both arms straight out in front. Tense your arm, shoulder and face muscles as tightly as possible. Exhale slowly, making a "sssshhh" sound, releasing the contraction and draining out the stress.

Balloon: Place your hands on top of your head, interlacing your fingers. Breathe in and raise your hands off your head with each puff of air. Take additional breaths through your nose as you raise your arms, blowing up an imaginary balloon. Release the air in the balloon by pursing your lips and exhaling slowly, lowering your hands and making a "pbpbpbpb" sound.

Pretzel: Stand or sit, crossing your right leg over your left leg at the ankles. Put your arms out in front and cross your right wrist over your left wrist. Turn your hands so your thumbs are pointing down. Put your palms together and interlace your fingers. Bend your elbows out and gently turn your hands down and toward your body until they rest on the center of your chest. Put your tongue on the roof of your mouth. Relax and breathe in this position.

The more you practice these calming strategies during times of relaxed alertness, the more accessible they will be during times of aroused emotional distress. At school, have children choose one of these calming strategies to do after each transition and whenever the classroom is becoming loud or disorganized. At home, have children choose one of these calming strategies to do after getting in the car, during a hectic morning experience, before starting their homework and at mealtimes (possibly before the blessing if that is a family tradition).

Downloading Calm

Emotions are contagious, as evidenced by the brain's mirror neuron system. The mirror neuron system allows us to see an emotion on someone's face and immediately sense that same emotion within ourselves. It allows for emotional communication and is essential to building empathy (Iacoboni, 2008). We've all had the experience where we walk into an office and everyone is miserable. In that emotional environment, how long does it take for you to begin complaining and feeling miserable yourself? When we become conscious of this dynamic, we can use it to promote a more positive atmosphere. When adults maintain a calm state while working or being with children, they can download that calm state into children. Focus on deep breathing and wishing well to achieve a peaceful internal state, and then use eye contact to download this state into the upset child. Instead of children downloading their upset to us, we can reverse the process and download our peace and calm to them.

Noticing

Emotions are biological and produce a universally common set of signals, as mentioned throughout this book. These signals include changes in facial expressions, tone of voice, action impulses, body posture, respiration, perspiration and increased cardiac activity (Ekman, 2003). In Conscious Discipline, this skill of describing these signals is called "noticing." When noticing a child, the adult describes what the child's body, arms and face are doing in order to bring the child's conscious awareness to his specific emotional state. This skill was demonstrated a great deal in Chapter 3.

The research behind conscious noticing is embedded in mindfulness. Mindfulness can be defined as an open and receptive attention to and awareness of what is occurring in the present moment (Black, 2011). Becoming mindful allows us to be the observer of our thoughts and feelings as well as the actions of others.

The basic noticing formula is the phrase, "Your _____ is going like this," accompanied by the physical modeling of the child's actions. "Your mouth is going like this." "Your face is going like this." Our job is to mirror the child's physical characteristics with calm and compassion. The slightest hint of mocking will derail the process entirely. Noticing must start in and come from your heart.

Noticing short-circuits our tendency to judge and stimulates the higher centers of the child's brain to come back online. As we mirror the child's physical state back to him with a helpful intent and without judgment, he will feel a natural tendency to look up at us. Once we regain eye contact we can reestablish our connection and download calm by taking a deep breath.

Sean wants to purchase some uncensored music from iTunes. His father catches him and loudly proclaims that such music will not be allowed! Sean immediately starts shaking his head side to side, crosses his hands tightly in front of him and presses his lips together. Dad notices the anger in his own voice and Sean's reaction. He starts taking deep, calming breaths to center himself. Sean turns away, wanting nothing to do with his father. Dad keeps breathing and notices Sean's reactions.

"You jerked around just like this (mirrors the movement). That's understandable. It's hard when you want something so badly. Your arms are crossed so tight, your knuckles are white like this (mirrors the movement)."

As Sean turns to see what Dad is doing, he makes eye contact. At that crucial point, Dad takes a deep breath, exhaling longer than he inhales. Due to the mirror neuron system, Sean unconsciously takes a deep breath, too. The small pause provided by the breath allows Sean the possibility of overcoming his triggers and maintaining the connection with his father so they can solve the problem.

In the above scene, Sean's dad used active calming and mirror neurons to facilitate the self-regulation process. He also used the key concepts of noticing and downloading. We can apply the same skills on a school playground:

Terri wants a turn on the swing. Miguel says, "No." Terri's fists clench, her lips narrow and her eyebrows pull down toward each other. The teacher, Mr. G, observes the whole scene. He consciously calms himself and approaches Terri.

Mr. G says, "Your hands are going like this (mirroring the action). Your face is going like this (mirroring the expression)."

Terri looks up at Mr. G. In that instant of connection, Mr. G takes a deep breath and Terri automatically starts breathing also. With the download complete, Mr. G quickly follows up with, "You seem angry. You wanted a turn on the swing. When Miguel said *no*, you didn't know what to do next. Tell Miguel, *I want a turn on the swing when you are finished*."

Terri speaks to Miguel, who turns his head away and slumps in his swing. Mr. G responds, "Your body went like this (mirrors the action) and you turned your head like this (mirrors the action). Miguel looks at Mr. G who instantly downloads calm and says, "Your body is telling me it's hard to take turns when you are having fun. I will set the timer and when the bell rings, it will be Terri's turn. You can do this, Miguel. You might be feeling disappointed, but you can handle it."

> Noticing helps children become aware of facial expressions and the non-verbal language of emotions. It teaches emotional literacy as children learn to read the faces of their friends and develop empathy.

During intense events, the adult's deep breathing and noticing may not seem powerful enough to break through to an extremely emotionally distressed child. During these times, it is helpful to ask the class to breathe as well. While visiting a classroom in Texas, a first grade child named Renee was having a complete meltdown because she did not finish her work in the allotted time. Her intense anger needed more than what the teacher could offer. This wise teacher used the entire School Family to help Renee start the self-regulation process.

> The School Family is a Conscious Discipline term used to describe a classroom of helpful, connected students.

"Boys and girls, Renee is having a difficult time. Let's all help her by taking three deep breaths." This shifts children's focus from what we don't want (the outburst) to what we do want (calm), while providing a way for each School Family member to actively contribute to the welfare of another. The teacher asked the class to put their hands on their hearts, take another deep breath and wish Renee well. These actions significantly increase the likelihood that Renee would pull herself together enough to continue her self-regulatory journey.

Malik has extensive sensory issues. During clean up time, a child knocks over several block structures, surprising two girls who start to scream. All this noise and activity puts Malik over the edge. He falls to the floor kicking and screaming. The teacher approaches Malik and notices his body. Her description only makes the tantrum worse. She takes a few deep breaths and says, "Breathe with me, Malik. You are safe." Again, this seems to offer no help. She elicits help from the classroom. "Children, Malik is having a hard time feeling safe right now. Let's all be a S.T.A.R. to help him." She leads the children in three deep S.T.A.R. breaths and in silently wishing him well. By the end of this process, Malik is able to organize himself just enough to stand up and make eye contact.

The teacher takes this opportunity to download calm, and then gently guide him to the classroom Safe Place where they continue active calming together.

I Am and I Calm: Goals

As we coach children through these first two steps in the self-regulation process, it is important to keep our eye on the following goals:

- Helping children recognize when they are triggered.
- Helping children understand they are lost when they are in the "I Am" state.
- Helping children learn to go to the Safe Place when feeling triggered.
- Helping children learn active calming activities to find themselves again.

Step 3: ❶ Feel

Naming the feeling. In the "I Feel" step, the adult identifies the feeling signals and names the feeling for the child with simple empathetic and informational (non-judgmental) language. The language we use with children during their emotional distress will become their inner speech and self-regulatory governing system. I would love to have a dime for every time I heard myself say to myself, "What were you thinking, Becky? You know better than that!" These words that I heard from the adults in my childhood did not help me calm down at age five any better than they did at age fifty-five. The language in the I Feel step is integral to helping children form helpful inner guidance and self-control.

Similar to the way a child uses your language to form his internal voice, he will use the same coaching language with his Buddy that you use with him. The skills the children teach to their Buddies reinforce the inner speech we are teaching them. It is a win-win cycle of self-control.

Helping the child name the feeling looks a little different during teachable moments and in the Safe Place, so let's look at these coaching methods separately.

I Feel: Teachable Moments

Emotional upset occurs all day with both adults and children. The adult's job is to keep the children safe physically, emotionally and socially. The children's job is to help keep the classroom, home, car and bus safe (Bailey, 2000). In order to be successful in their jobs, both adults and children must manage their emotions in an effective way. This emotional management is essential because it is the bridge between problem and solution. As conflict emerges, adults must address the emotional state first and the behavior second. I repeat this phrase throughout this book because it is so essential. If we do not address the emotional upset first and the behavior second, we end up sacrificing our relationship with others in order to set limits. As our relationship becomes more negative than positive, the child's willingness to solve problems begins to dissipate and eventually power struggles are all that will remain.

In the I Feel step, the adult identifies the feeling signals and names the feeling for the child with a basic formula that mimics the Describe, Name, Acknowledge (DNA) script from Chapter 3:

Describe: "Your face is going like this."

Name: "You seem _____?" (Fill in the emotional word and say this with a questioning tone.)

Acknowledge: If you did not witness the event, ask, "Something happened?" If you witnessed the event, you would make your best guess at acknowledging what the child wanted by saying, "You wanted _____," or "You were hoping _____."

Activity

Fill in the blanks in the activity below to practice coaching children through their distressed emotional states.

Scene 1: An Angry Child

Description: Someone took the seat next to the teacher.

"Your _____ is going like this. Your _____ is going like this."
Wait for eye contact then download.
"Breathe with me."
"You seem _____. You wanted _____."
"It's hard. You were hoping to _____."

"You have a choice. You may sit across from the teacher so you can see each other or you may sit next to Taite. What is your choice? Breathe, you can handle this."

Scene 2: A Sad Child

Description: Her cat just died.

"Your _____ is going like this. Your _____ is going like this."
"You seem _____. You were hoping _____
_____."

"It's hard. We will get through this together."

Hopefully you are getting a sense for how helpful it will be to use the DNA script you learned in Chapter 3 and apply it to situations where the child is upset.

I Feel: Safe Place

When children come to the Safe Place, they are generally in the I Am state of becoming the emotion. Their first activity is to begin the I Calm step in the self-regulation process. After a few deep breaths or other calming option, the child selects the Buddy or emotional recognition doll that best represents how she is feeling. The adult then coaches the child to help her Buddy self-regulate its emotions. The goal is for you to teach the child, and for the child to teach her Buddy the same self-regulatory skills.

Teach the child to help her Buddy self-regulate by using language that is almost identical to the process used in teachable moments. For example, when coaching sadness, encourage the child to say the following to her Sad Feeling Buddy:

"Hello Sad."
"Welcome Sad."

"Your eyes are going like this (child models for Buddy)."
"Your mouth is going like this (child models for Buddy)."

"You seem sad (strokes and soothes the Buddy)."

"Breathe with me, Sad (teaches Buddy how to breathe)."

"You can handle this (hugs and comforts Buddy)."
"You are safe!"

The *Feeling Buddies DVDs*, part of the complete *Feeling Buddies Self-Regulation Toolkits for Parents* and *Educators*, shows Ms. Valero coaching children through the five-step self-regulation process in the Safe Place. Teaching the language and skills this way might feel awkward at first, but as you see the expressions on the child's face and the resulting ease you experience in your discipline approach, it will be well worth the effort to make the life changes.

I Feel: Goals

As we coach the child through the I Feel step of the self-regulation process, it is important to keep the following goals in mind:

- Children internalize the language we use as we respond to their emotional distress, especially during teachable moments. This language ultimately becomes the children's inner speech and self-regulatory system for the rest of their lives.
- Children will use the same coaching language with the Feeling Buddies that we use with them, reinforcing the same inner speech.

Step 4: 🄸 Choose

Accept and reframe. When we name and identify our feelings, we are less likely to wallow in them or rant and rave about them. Remember, emotions are the bridge between a problem and its solution. The goal is not to get on the bridge and just stand there. The goal is to walk across the bridge from problem to solution.

Naming the feeling is not enough; we must also completely embrace the feeling state. Identifying a feeling and then saying to ourselves, *"You shouldn't feel like this,"* blocks our wisdom. Instead, we must welcome our feelings and lean into them. We also must be willing to allow them to stay as long as necessary; a scary proposition for many of us. The irony is that allowing something to be also allows it to leave.

There is a "Hello Song" on the *Listen to Your Feelings* music CD that says, "Stay by my side for as long as you want." To do this, we must accept *what is* and let go of what we think *should be*. Acceptance empowers us to embrace the feeling, regulate its intensity and return our internal state to one of calm and happiness. We are able to see the problem from different perspectives when we return to an integrated coherent state of calm. This automatically allows us to reframe the situation in a new more hopeful light. We can shift from what we *don't* want to what we *do* want, bringing solutions into focus.

In the I Choose step, the adult responds to the underlying message of the child's emotion first and then addresses the behavioral needs of the situation. We must understand and attune with the underlying message so we can respond to the emotion appropriately. Attunement requires we understand the child's inner world and mirror it back to her so she can make sense of it herself. Common messages were introduced in Chapter 3 and are revisited below:

Anger and Frustration's message is "Someone or something is getting in my way." When a child pushes another child off the chair, choose to address the theme of the feeling instead of saying, "Was that nice? What is our rule about pushing?"

> *"You wanted a turn with the computer and didn't know the words to use. When you want a turn, tap Erin on the shoulder, call her name and say, 'Erin, I would like a turn on the computer.'"*

Scared and Anxious' message is one of threat. When a child is anxious about completing a work assignment, choose to address the theme instead of saying, "Get busy. You are going to run out of time."

> *"You're safe. Breathe. You have twenty minutes left. Keep breathing. If you need help, raise your hand like this."*

Sadness and Disappointment's message is about loss. As a child is sad about a friend moving to another city, choose to address the theme instead of saying, "It will be fine. You can email each other. You'll make a new best friend."

"It's hard to lose a friend. I am here for you. You just cry. We will get through this together. It is hard and you can handle this."

Happiness and Calm's message is about extending and sharing. As a child is excited about the lizard she found, choose to address the theme instead of saying, "Don't bring that thing in this house! It's great you found it but you are scaring it to death. Go put it back outside."

"What a find! Tell me all about it as we work together to keep the lizard safe."

As stated in Chapter 1 and repeated often, a founding principle of the five-step self-regulation process is "What you offer to others, you strengthen within yourself." If we offer others our judgment, we will feel not good enough. If we offer others love and acceptance, we will feel good enough and confident enough to move forward in our own lives. As I write this book, I strengthen my own emotional wellbeing. As you coach children with these techniques, you strengthen the same skills within yourself. As children tend to their Feeling Buddies, they teach themselves the accepting and embracing process, too.

I Choose: Teachable Moments

Positive intent is the willingness to see the best in others at all times. It is looking past the behavior and seeing the essence of children, knowing they are doing the best they can in a given moment. Offering positive intent is a choice and an act of love. Seeing the best is easy when others look like you, act like you and think like you. It becomes harder when we believe others are behaving inappropriately, disrespectfully or aggressively (Bailey, 2000). We must offer positive intent if we expect children to move from being stuck in the problem to reaching forward toward solutions.

Positive intent asks us to mirror back to the child what we believe she truly wants, not what she is currently doing. We must be willing to look beyond her negative behavior to see the true need, whether it's the need to belong, exert power, have fun, gain freedom or survive. Once we acknowledge what the child wants, we can then set a limit or provide alternatives.

Luis wants to sit by the teacher. When he hears the signal to come to circle, he runs across the room, pushes Amber away from the spot next to the teacher and proudly plops himself down. His teacher has a choice at this moment. She can focus on the rules (no running, no pushing). She can focus on the pain Luis caused Amber ("Look how you *made* Amber feel! Would you like people to treat you like that?"). She could offer positive intent to Luis, building a bridge between the problem and the solution ("You wanted to sit by my side, so you ran across the room and pushed Amber to get the perfect seat. You may not push your friends or run. It is not safe. When you want to sit next to me, you must say to Amber, *Would you please move?*").

Be certain to state the child's desire and the acceptable behavior in positive form. For emotions to finish their journey from unconscious sensation to conscious integration, we must focus on what we want rather than what we don't want. For example:

Child: "I don't want to sit here."
Teacher: "You wanted to choose your own seat this morning."

Child: "I hate reading!"
Teacher: "You seem so frustrated. You were hoping center time would last longer."

Child: "You are always picking on me. You never pick on Emma!"
Parent: "You seem frustrated. You were hoping we could have some time just the two of us today."

Child: "Are we having beans again?"
Parent: "You were hoping we would have something different for dinner tonight."

Children who are learning to regulate their emotions or who have difficulty with self-regulation need to be reminded they are safe. A simple reassurance, "You are safe. Breathe with me. You can handle this," is extremely helpful. Children who have not received feedback from an attuned adult have not learned that the emotional distress they are feeling is like a weather pattern and will pass. The sun *will* shine again and every attuned adult is a ray of light.

I Choose: In the Safe Place

Acceptance leads to integration and integration leads to choice. In the Safe Place, it is critical to provide visual choices to help children calm and relax their systems enough to change their feeling state from upset to calm. The choices could be specific to one child or broad enough for the whole class or for all siblings. You can create these visual choices yourself, utilize the choice cards in the *Brain Smart Choices for Connection and Calming* or employ the *I Choose: Self-Control Board*. These helpful tools can be purchased on the Conscious Discipline website. Choices you may wish to use in your Safe Place include:

- Extended techniques for calming (other than S.T.A.R., drain, balloon, pretzel). This might include Bunny Breathing or Seated Cobra stretch.

Bunny Breathing: Hold one hand up with two fingers standing tall like a peace sign to represent the bunny. The tall fingers are the ears and the balled hand is the bunny body. Scrunch up your nose and take three short breaths. As you do this, have the bunny's ears go up and down with the breathing. Hold your breath for three seconds and then exhale slowly, moving your hand across your body as if the bunny is hopping away. Try to exhale as long as the bunny is hopping.

Seated Cobra: Sit in your chair with your legs apart and one hand on each knee. Starting from a relaxed position, breathe in and lower your shoulders down and forward, then breathe out and roll forward and up, arching your back and looking toward the ceiling. When you have stretched as far as you can, breathe to the count of three and hiss like a snake on the exhale.

- Activities for connecting with the adult or the Buddy: Cranky Cream, Story Hand, Twinkle, Twinkle and other I Love You Rituals (Bailey, 2000).

Story Hand: *I Love You Rituals page 167*
Tell the child, "It is story time." The child will probably think you are going to read a book. Instead, take his/her hand and tell a reassuring or encouraging story about a success, concern or event in the child's day.

Start with the pinky finger, giving it a nice massage and saying, "This little finger wanted to learn how to ride a two-wheel bicycle." (The story you tell will be based on your child's life.) Go to the next finger and give it a massage, saying, "This finger was a little afraid that he might fall off." Continue to the next finger, saying, "But this finger said, 'I can do it. I just know I can.'" At the index finger, continue "So he decided to try and try again." Finally, massage the thumb and say excitedly, "Did he do it? Did he do it?" Then tuck the thumb into the palm of the child's hand make a reassuring or *You did it*-type statement: "No problem. All the fingers knew she would do it all the time."

Twinkle, Twinkle: *I Love You Rituals page 63, Songs for I Love You Rituals Volume 1*
Twinkle, twinkle, little star,
What a wonderful child you are!
With bright eyes and nice round cheeks,
Talented person from head to feet.
Twinkle, twinkle, little star,
What a wonderful child you are!

- Activities for reflection: Writing, drawing or talking.

I Love You Rituals and other connection activities are essential to use in the Safe Place and to conduct during whole group instruction on a daily basis. The I Love You Rituals activities promote willingness and build your School Family so children are more likely to choose to go to the Safe Place than to be disruptive.

I Choose: Goals

As we coach the child through the I Choose step of the self-regulation process, it is important to keep our eye on the following goals:

- Accepting our feelings allows for choice. Providing choices for children to finish their self-regulation journey is vital for changing the internal state from upset to calm.
- Offering positive intent to children teaches them to offer positive intent to themselves and others by reframing the situation in a new perspective.
- Conducting connection activities. These are helpful for self-regulation because they promote the willingness and cooperation to solve the problem instead of sliding back into blame.

In this step, children are able to talk about the situation that triggered their upset. They are also able to hear additional information from the adult and gain deeper insight into the situation. This information is helpful and leads the child gracefully into the final step of problem-solving.

Step 5: 🅘 Solve

Solutions. In the final step, the bridge has been crossed and the child is ready to address the problem. Problem-solving requires we revisit the trigger with a new perspective, skill and willingness. If we have completed the first four steps, we will be guided toward a win-win solution for all involved. The solution always reinforces the self-regulation steps and strengthens connections with others. If we approach problems from an unregulated state; however, win-win solutions are impossible to find, and we become mired in the win-lose paradigm of power struggles and temporary fixes. Win-win solutions generally will fall into one of the following categories:

- Conflict resolution.
- Accepting the current feeling state as one you can tolerate and manage.
- Learning a new skill.
- Visually structuring the environment for success.
- Establishing stronger connections.

Conflict Resolution

Elizabeth and Blake get into a tussle on the playground. Both tempers run high. After calming down, they both are willing to resolve their conflict by using the *I Solve: Conflict Resolution Time Machine* mat. The *Time Machine* is a structure that helps adults and children transform aggressive acts into life lessons through respectful, assertive communication. It is the hub of the bully prevention program in an early childhood classroom and key to teaching respectful assertiveness at home. The *Time Machine* has footprints that lead the two children (aggressor and victim) through seven steps that teach them to assertively handle aggression and printed words that help the adult coach the interaction. It provides a teachable moment for the whole class and is an excellent way to help siblings resolve their squabbles. To learn more about this structure, visit Shubert's Classroom on the Conscious Discipline website and watch the *Time Machine* in action.

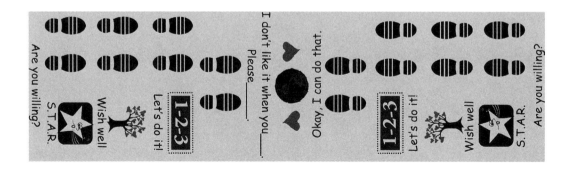

Accepting the Current Feeling State

Often we don't think of managing our own feelings as a solution; however, it is a powerful one. In situations like divorce or the death of a dog, there is no tangible solution to the problem. These situations require vigilance in managing your emotions well enough to function as best as is possible. Many people attending my workshops would be surprised to know that I used to leave my cell phone on during my presentations. For years, I was responsible for the care for my ailing parents and was to be called in case of emergencies. I could do this because I was able to manage the anxiety of knowing the phone might ring at any time and the emotions that would bubble up when it did. I could conduct a workshop with the feeling of fear by my side. The Feeling Buddies empower children who are going through difficult life journeys to cope with them. The "I'm safe. Keep breathing. I can handle this" language is extremely powerful for both adults and children when it is said from the heart.

Learning a New Skill

Stefano learned to use his BIG voice when he was pushed away from the water fountain. He would say to his peers in an assertive voice, "I don't like it when you push me. Get behind me and wait your turn." On this particular day, he assertively spoke up, but Darius did not listen. Stefano was flooded with anger, but was able to walk away from the situation and go to the Safe Place. In the Safe Place, his teacher coached him through the self-regulation steps and in learning the new skill of "asking for help." They decided if the other children did not listen to him, Stefano would go to the teacher and say, "I need some help. My friends are not listening to me."

Visually Structuring the Environment for Success

Thia has a hard time remembering to put the papers she is taking home into her backpack and remembering to bring them back to school the next day. She often feels sad for losing out on opportunities like field trips because she has forgotten permission slips. She also feels angst over not turning her work in on time. These triggers send her to the Safe Place. After moving through her self-regulation steps, she and the teacher decided to implement a picture outline for a routine she will follow at school. They tape this visual routine to her seat. The teacher encourages Thia to go through her steps at the end of each school day. She also sent a similar visual system for Thia to use at home.

Establishing Stronger Connections

Amanda would cry every day at rest time and lunch. She also had problems separating from Mom in the mornings. Her teacher, Mrs. Ruffo, knew this could be a sign of attachment triggers. After coaching Amanda to use the Safe Place to self-regulate, she and Amanda came up with a plan they thought would be helpful. First, Mrs. Ruffo planned a home visit so Amanda would see Mom and Mrs. Ruffo interacting together. Then Mrs. Ruffo began to connect with Amanda each day by doing an I Love You Ritual. This sparked a growth spurt in their relationship. Finally, Mrs. Ruffo helped Amanda make a small book of family photos. Whenever Amanda felt the need, she could hold and look at the picture book.

Moving Forward

Our feelings serve a vital role in our development. They focus our attention, alerting and motivating us to take action. They are social signals that communicate and link us with others. They are the bridge between problem and solutions. They guide all our decision making, whether conscious or unconscious. The following chart summarizes the five steps of self-regulation, the coaching goals and the strategies adults must provide for children in order to make the most of their feelings.

Five Steps of Self-Regulation	Coaching Goals	Coaching Strategies
Step 1: **🅘 Am**	I Am state = I am lost. Help children recognize their triggers. Teach children to go to the Safe Place when triggered.	Change the environment. Change your response. Teach acceptable ways to get needs met. Compassion, calming and problem-solving: "You're safe. Breathe with me." Teach children to go to the Safe Place when triggered.
Step 2: **🅘 Calm**	Calming strategies = I am found. Active calming: Practice the four core strategies throughout the day. Download calm with eye contact. Noticing: Describe and demonstrate emotional facial signals and body language.	S.T.A.R. Drain Balloon Pretzel "Your eyebrows are going like this."

Five Steps of Self-Regulation	Coaching Goals	Coaching Strategies
Step 3:  **Feel**	Address emotional signals and states first, behavior changes second. Help children coach their Buddies. Relate your responses back to the generic theme of the feelings. Anger = You wanted something you didn't get. Scared = You felt threatened and need safety/protection. Sad = You lost something dear to you. We'll get through it together. It's hard. Happy = You want me to be present with you. We can join together and connect.	"Your face is going like this. You seem angry. You wanted her to move. You didn't know the words to use. Tell Jill, *Move over please.*" "Hello Anger, Welcome Anger. Your eyes are going like this. Your mouth is going like this." (Child models for Buddy.) "You seem angry." (Child strokes and soothes her Buddy.) "Breathe with me, Anger." (Child teaches her Buddy how to breathe.) "You can handle this! You are safe." Child hugs and comforts his Buddy.) "Breathe with me. (Child breathes with his Buddy on his chest.)

Five Steps of Self-Regulation	Coaching Goals	Coaching Strategies
Step 4: 	Offer positive intent to aggressive behavior to reframe the situation for all. Create choices for the class and individual children. The choices relate back to your observation. Create class-made/home-made books to help children see the positive consequences of healthy choices.	Approach aggressor with "You wanted _____" or "You were hoping _____" in order to teach a new skill. Stock your Safe Place with props for different calming choices. Include I Love You Ritual options and cranky cream. Provide visuals of choices that are acceptable.

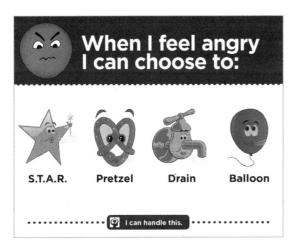

Five Steps of Self-Regulation	Coaching Goals	Coaching Strategies
Step 5:  **Solve**	Coach child to discover win-win solutions. Structure situations to help children resolve conflicts. Relate the solutions back to the triggers.	Teach a new skill. Add pictures to help children learn solution steps. Accept the current feeling state as one that is tolerable and manageable. "You can handle this." Visually structure the environment for success. Establish stronger connections with I Love You Rituals and other bonding activities. Utilize the *I Solve: Conflict Resolution Time Machine*.

For many of you, the information in this book inspires you to delve deeper into the self-regulation journey and you are ready to implement the full *Feeling Buddies Toolkit* in your home or classroom. As you begin to implement the complete toolkit, allow the activities within it to spark your own brilliance. It's vital that you learn the five-step process for yourself, and then teach from your heart rather than prescriptively going from point to point. Most importantly, let your awareness be a gift for change and allow your creativity to lead the way. My intent is that this book and the *Feeling Buddies Toolkits* spur dramatic changes that will transform every facet of your life. Breathe deeply, see each moment as an opportunity to learn, and have fun!

For others, this is where I leave you. You have learned what research says about self-regulation, explored factors that block our ability to self-regulate, discovered ways to self-regulate as an adult and learned ways to help children self-regulate. Perhaps you feel this book has given you plenty of strategies to play with, or you've simply learned enough for now. Whatever the reason, I hope you have found this text both enjoyable and insightful, and encourage you to practice its teachings in your everyday life. I wish you well in your journey.

Just one more thing before I go... a special surprise just for you! Each of the four core Feeling Buddies has written you a personal note. They wanted to extend their hands in friendship before you begin. They need you and you need them. Enjoy!

My dearest one,

Hello. I would like to introduce myself. I am your Feeling Buddy, Sad. I am a part of you. I come to you when you have lost something you love and value. We have met before.

A lot of people don't like my visits. Sometimes, I only get to peek in the door before someone stuffs cookies in my mouth. Sometimes I have a glass of wine in one hand and a credit card in the other. It's hard to hug you when my hands are full! Please don't feed me, get me drunk, buy me more stuff or lose me in your work. I have a job to do. I help you let go. I would like for you to accept me, love me, listen to me and embrace me into your wholeness. I don't like sleeping on the porch. Please let me in.

It's hard to lose people, pets, relationships and opportunities. It's hard when children grow up and start making their own lives. It's difficult when things don't turn out the way you thought they would. I come to help you express those losses and realize that love is all that is real. Without our time together, you can't move forward through your losses. Trying to hang onto things and people is impossible. You already know that on some level, so what do you say? Let's be buddies!

Here is what I need from you:
- Uncover all the ways you try to keep me on the front porch rather than inviting me in.
- Please acknowledge and welcome me. A simple, "Welcome, Sad. Come on in. We can get through this loss together," would be helpful.
- Breathe into me and say, "Hello, Sadness." Then we can sit side by side. When I first show up, it's really difficult because you and I become one. I promise you, it will not be like that for long. I am me and you are you. I will be beside you only as long as you need to work through the loss.

- Be aware when you have become me. Becoming me feels like you are drowning in a lake of tears. For us to have a healthy relationship, you must name me, feel me and get out of the lake. I have some messages for you, but you can't hear them when you are under water. Please move from "I am sad" to "I feel sad" so you can listen to my tender guidance.
- Carry me around with you. Ask me, "Sad, would you like to go to work today?" Listen for my answer; don't assume you know. If the answer is "Yes," take my hand and let's go. Please don't abandon me or set me aside. When you ignore or dismiss me, I spend all my time trying to get your attention. How exhausting! Breathe into me and accept me so you can start healing.

I want you to know that as we learn to trust each other, you will be able to hear the important and healing messages I have for you. Please give me a chance to do my job by delivering those messages. I hope you will listen because I love you oodles and beyond.

Love,
Your Feeling Buddy, Sad

My beloved one,

Let me introduce myself. My name is Angry and I am a part of you. I would like for you to accept me, love me, listen to me and embrace me into your wholeness. Until now, you have not treated me well. I have tried over and over through the years to get your attention and give you some important messages. In turn, you have treated me like the evil stepsisters treated Cinderella.

I am excited that we will finally spend some time together. I am a wonderful Feeling Buddy; you just haven't given me much of a chance to prove it to you. I have a job to do. I motivate you to change. Sometimes you might need to change a relationship, let go of limiting beliefs or change a job. You might need to change how you see things. Or you might need to change how you respond to me showing up within you.

Here is what I need from you:
* Acknowledge my existence. A simple, "Hello, Angry," when I show up will make a world of difference for you and me.
* Feel me and then quickly help me because we become one when I first show up. Don't stay one with me for long; I am me and you are you. I am a powerful energy. I can rush blood to your head, heat up your hands, increase your breathing and beat your heart so hard you can hear it! I'm a wonderful force for good, but if you become me,

ignore me or bury me, I become a nasty storm that shuts down your heart and closes you off from your true self and others.

*   Become aware of my presence before I take charge of you. I am quick, so you must really get to know me and what triggers me within you.

*   Breathe with me and sometimes for me. Remember, I am a powerful force and I depend on you to help me regulate my arousal so I'm not hurtful to others or you. I don't like being hurtful. I like to motivate, not destroy.

*   Own me instead of turning me into judgments and outbursts against others. Calm me down so you can hear my message. We can do this!

As we start to trust each other, you'll see that my messages are about helping you change. Will you listen? I hope so because I love you heaps and bunches.

Love,
Your Feeling Buddy,
Anger

My adored one,

Hello. I would like to introduce myself. I am your Feeling Buddy, Scared. I come to you when your safety is threatened. I am a part of you, the part of you that wants to live and survive anything. I will always guide you to withdraw from a situation but never ask you to withdraw from love.

Like anger, I am a powerful force. You might like me because I make your heart race to bring you to high alert when you nearly fall asleep while driving. You might not like me because I keep you from doing things you want to do but feel too scared to try. Misunderstanding me can keep you in unhealthy relationships and situations, afraid to leave. I can dampen your love for life if you let me overgrow like a weed.

You and I become one when I first appear. If we stay as one too long, I will destroy your immune system, deteriorate your joints and eat away at your brain. I don't really want to move in and be one with you. I'm a short-visit kind of Feeling Buddy. I just want to pop in, save your life and leave! You might call me the best relative you ever had: I want to show up on time, deliver my helpful message and quickly depart. (This is not true of the rest of my family. My cousins, Worry and Anxious, come for a day and stay for years because they hang out in the past and the future. You never can find them in the present moment, so it's hard to pack their bags and show them the door.)

My message is simple. I want you to seek safety and protection, and I want you to do it now. I guess you could call me the ultimate Safekeeper.

Here is what I need from you:
- Listen to me, pay attention, take action and then release me to take care of other 911 calls.

- Seek safety, but choose your safety wisely. If you think safety is drugs, alcohol, television, food, edgy sex or made up stories (like "The only person I can trust is myself"), then you are in trouble. The safety I ask you to seek always helps you feel better in both the short and long term. If you feel better briefly and then feel worse, or if you feel a little better but have a nagging feeling something's not right, then you haven't really listened to my message.

- Release me. Don't be one with me for long. I can be toxic. When we stay as one I will distort your worldview. The chemicals I release are perfect for fight or flight, but they damage your body and mind when allowed to stay too long. If you are in chronic pain, have an unfulfilled life or suffer from disease, we may have spent too much time together as one.

- Relax after my visit. Take a vacation, read a good book and shower love on everyone you know. Above all, be grateful that I came and went.

Trust me. I am on your side. Survival is our goal and if you are reading this, we have done well together. I hope you will listen to my message because I love you for lifetimes of lifesavers!

Love,
Your Feeling Buddy,
Scared

My dear honey bunny,

Hello! I would like to introduce myself to you. I am your Feeling Buddy, "Happy." You might be thinking, "I know you, we've had some fun times." I'm not sure you truly do know me. I am the core of who you are. I am the Buddy who knows (without any doubt) that all things are good, happen for good and bring more good.

I think a lot of people confuse me with pleasure. Pleasure is a rip-roaring moment that makes for a great memory. It feels good, but is fleeting. I feel good, peaceful and loving, and I never leave. If this were baseball, I would be your dugout. If this were the sea, I would be the water. If this were a community, I would be your home.

Take a few deep breaths to connect with nature, the divine force you believe in or your loved ones, and watch me come into your awareness. Hi! That's me!

It's important for you to you know me. As you run to seek happiness, I run behind you, hoping you will know I'm right there. You can't buy me, win me or obtain me. I am not a bigger house or a smaller waistline. I am simply the choice you can make to recognize me.

To make that choice, here is what I need from you:
- Believe me when I tell you that your natural state is one of love and happiness.
- Stop looking for me out there. Look within. I'm always there waiting with a cute little grin you can't help but recognize! I'm soft and comforting. Feel free to cuddle up with me.

- Find out what blocks your awareness of me. Your insecurities about deserving and worthiness push me away. Your seeking of money, things and the perfect body hide my face from you. All that stuff about being stupid or smart, tall or short, black or white, gay or straight just muffles my sweet voice. I am the loving spirit you have stifled, pushed away, covered and sold out. Let all that go; all is well. I'm right here!

- Please choose me over pleasure. I'm not better than pleasure, it's just that pleasure comes with pain. I am a solo act, and I encompass everything. You can't miss with me; I am pain-free.

All you have to do is relax into me. Know that love (my main squeeze) is the most powerful force. Once you share me with others, there is nothing we can't do together. I call that fun. I call you Honey Bunny! What do you say? Are you in?

Loving you as if you were me,
Your Feeling Buddy, Happy

Feeling Buddies Sample Curriculum

Lesson 1.1

Goal: Introduce Happy and Sad Feeling Buddies
Song: **It's Buddy Time**

It's Buddy Time
(Sing to tune of Did You Ever See a Lassie)

It's time to get the Buddies,
The Buddies, the Buddies,
It's time to get the Buddies,
The Feeling Buddies now.
So sit in the circle and
Get ready to listen,
It's time to get the Buddies,
Take a breath and look at me.

Teacher: I have really been looking forward to our lesson today! I am going to introduce some new friends to you. They are called our Feeling Buddies and they will be very helpful in our classroom. (Keep Happy and Sad Feeling Buddies hidden behind your back, under a blanket or in a basket.) Before I introduce them to you, I have a question for you. Have you ever felt happy?
Children respond.
Teacher: We have all had times that we felt happy. This is one of our new friends, Happy. (Hold up the Happy Feeling Buddy.) One of my happiest moments was... (share a personal story).

Buddy Tip: When sharing stories with children it is best to share authentic stories from your own lives. Authentic stories help build connections. Make sure your stories are developmentally appropriate for your children. It is also helpful to have a talking stick or toy microphone to indicate who is talking.

Teacher: Look at Happy's eyebrows. They are going like this (demonstrate). Look at his mouth. It is going like this (demonstrate). Make your face look like Happy's face.
Children respond.
Teacher: You did it. Your eyebrows are going like this (demonstrate). Your mouth is going like this (demonstrate). You seem happy, just like our new Feeling Buddy friend. I see your faces like this every day. It is exciting!
Happy: (Use Happy like a puppet.) Hi everyone! I am so excited to meet you and be with you. We will have fun together! You know what I like to say a lot? "Yahoo, look at you. Happy, happy, clap, one, two." Say it with me and clap your hands. Watch me; I'll show you. Yahoo, look at you. Happy, happy, clap, one, two.
Teacher: (Place Happy in your lap.) I have another question for you. Have you ever felt sad? (Bring out the Sad Feeling Buddy and hold it up.)
Children respond.

Teacher: Look at Sad's eyebrows. They are going like this (demonstrate). Look at his mouth. It is going like this (demonstrate). Can you make your face look like his?

Children respond.

Teacher: You did it. Your eyebrows are going like this (demonstrate). Your mouth is going like this (demonstrate). You seem sad just like our new Feeling Buddy friend. There are times I have seen this look on your faces, just like there are times I've seen your happy faces!

Sad: (Using Sad like a puppet.) Hi everyone, my name is Sad. I help people when they lose something they love. I will always help you. When I show up, your face looks just like mine.

Teacher: (Put Sad in your lap with Happy.) I'm going to teach you a new song about feeling happy and sad.

Song: Look at my Face Part 1

Buddy Tip:
Hold up each Feeling Buddy as you sing.

Look at my Face Part 1
(Sing to the tune of When the Saints Go Marching In)

Look at my face (echo),
Look at my face (echo),
Look at my face when I feel happy.
When I feel happy,
I look like this.
This is my face when I feel happy.
(All children make the face)
Look at my face (echo),
Look at my face (echo),
Look at my face when I feel sad.
When I feel sad,
I look like this.
This is my face when I feel sad.
(All children make the face)

Happy: (Use Happy like a puppet.) Bye, everyone. Yahoo, look at you. Happy, happy, clap, one, two.

Sad: (Use Sad like a puppet.) Bye bye!

Children respond.

Teacher: Happy and Sad live in these pockets. (Show children the Feeling Buddies Pockets. Put Happy and Sad in their places.) Look boys and girls, their names are on their pockets. (Point to the words and read the names with the children.) We have met two of our eight new friends. Once we meet all eight of them, they will help us be loving and kind to each other.

Song: Bye Bye Buddies

Bye Bye Buddies
(Sing to the tune of Goodnight Ladies)

Bye bye Buddies,
Bye bye Buddies,
Bye bye Buddies,
We will meet again.

References

Arnold, D. H., McWilliams, L., & Arnold, E. H. (1998) Teacher discipline and child misbehavior in preschool: Untangling causality with correlational data. *Developmental Psychology*, 34, 276-287.

Bailey, B. A., (1997). *I Love You Rituals: Activities to Build Bonds and Strengthen Relationships With Children.* New York: Harper Collins.

Bailey, B. A. (2000) *Conscious Discipline: 7 Skills for Brain Smart Classroom Management.* Oviedo, FL: Loving Guidance, Inc.

Bailey, B. A. (2000) *Easy to Love, Difficult to Discipline: The 7 Basic Skills for Turning Conflict into Cooperation.* New York: Harper Collins.

Bailey, B. A. (2011) *Creating the School Family: Bully-Proofing Classrooms Through Emotional Intelligence.* Oviedo, FL: Loving Guidance, Inc.

Black, D.S. (2011) A brief definition of mindfulness. *Mindfulness Research Guide.* Retrieved from: http://www.mindfulexperience.org.

Boyd, J., Barnett, W. S., Bodrova, E., Leong, D. J., & Gomby, D. (2005) Promoting children's social and emotional development through preschool. New Brunswick, NJ: NIERR. Retrieved from: http://nieerorg/resources/policyreports/report7.pdf.

Bronson, M. B. (2000) *Self-Regulation in Early Childhood: Nature and Nurture.* New York: The Guilford Press.

Bronson, P. & Merryman, A. (2009) *NurtureShock: New Thinking about Children.* New York: Twelve Hachette Book Club.

Damasio, A. R. (1999) The Feeling of What Happens: Body and Emotion in the Making of Consciousness. Orlando, FL: Harcourt.

Decety, J. & Hodges, S. D. (2006) A social cognitive neuroscience model of human empathy. In P.A.M. van Lange (Ed.), *Bridging Social Psychology: Benefits of Transdisciplinary Approaches* (pp. 103-109). Mahwah, NJ: Lawrence Erlbaum Associates.

Eisenberg, N., Spinrad, T. L., Fabes, R. A., Reiser, M., Cumberland, A., Shepard, S. A., Thompson, M. (2004) The relations of effortful control and impulsivity to children's resiliency and adjustment. *Child Development*, 75(1), 25-46.

Ekman, P. (2003) *Emotions Revealed: Recognizing Faces and Feelings to Improve Communication and Emotional Life.* New York: Henry Holt and Company.

Gilliam, W. S. (2005) Prekindergarteners Left Behind: Expulsion Rates in State Prekindergarten Systems. New Haven, CT: Yale University Child Study Center.

Goleman, D. (1995) *Emotional Intelligence.* New York: Bantam Books.

Goleman, D. (1998) *Working with Emotional Intelligence.* New York: Bantam Books.

Gottman, J. M., Katz, L. F., & Hooven, C. (1996) Parental meta-emotion philosophy and the emotional life of families: Theoretical models and preliminary data. *Journal of Family Psychology*, 10, 243–268.

Greenberg, M. T., & Snell, J. L. (1997) Brain development and emotional development: The role of teaching in organizing the frontal lobe. In P. Salovey, D. J. Sluyter, P. Salovey, & D. J. Sluyter (Eds.), *Emotional Development and Emotional Intelligence: Educational Implications* (pp. 93–126). New York: Basic Books.

Hastings, R. P. (2003) Child Behavior Problems and Partner Mental Health as Correlates of Stress in Mothers and Fathers of Children with Autism. *Journal of Intellectual Disability Research*, 47: 231-7.

Huffman, L. C., Mehlinger, S. L., & Kerivan, A. S. (2001) Risk factors for academic and behavioral problems in the beginning of school. In Off to a good start: Research on the risk factors for early school problems and selected federal policies affecting children's social and emotional development and their readiness for school. Chapel Hill, NC: University of North Carolina, FPG Child Development Center.

Iacoboni, M. (2008) *Mirroring People: The New Science of how we Connect with Others.* New York: Farrar, Straus and Giroux.

Kanat-Maymon M., & Assor, A. (2010) Perceived maternal control and responsiveness to distress as predictors of young adults' empathic responses. *Personality and Social Psychology Bulletin*, 36, 33–46.

Katz, L. F., & Gottman, J. M., (1994) Patterns of marital interaction and children's emotional development. In R. D. Parke and S. G. Kellam (Eds.), *Exploring Family Relationships with Other Social Contexts*, Ch. 3, (pp. 49-74). Hillsdale, NJ: Lawrence Erlbaum.

Kessler, R. C., Chiu, W. T., Demler, O., & Walters, E. E. (2005) Prevalence, severity, and comorbidity of twelve-month DSM-IV disorders in the National Comorbidity Survey Replication (NCS-R). *Archives of General Psychiatry*, 62: 617-627.

Kranowitz, C. (1998) *The Out-of-Sync Child: Recognizing and Coping with Sensory Integration Dysfunction*. New York: Perigee Trade.

Kupersmidt, J. B., Bryant, D., & Willoughby, M. T. (2000) Prevalence of aggressive behaviors among preschoolers in Head Start and community child care programs. *Behavioral Disorders*, 26: 42-52.

Lunkenheimer, E. S., Shields, A. M., & Cortina, K. S. (2007) Parental coaching and dismissing of children's emotions in family interaction. *Social Development*, 16(2), 232-248.

Lyon, G. R. & Krasnegor, N. A. (1996) *Attention, Memory and Executive Function*. Baltimore: Paul H. Brookes.

Nagin, D. S. & Tremblay, R. E. (1999) Trajectories of boys' physical aggression, opposition and hyperactivity on the path to physically violent and nonviolent juvenile delinquency. *Child Development*, 70(5), 1181-1196.

National Council on Developing Child. (2005) Children's Emotional Development is Built into the Architecture of Their Brains. Retrieved from: http://www.developingchild.net.

Ohman, A. (2000) Fear and anxiety: Clinical, evolutionary, and cognitive perspectives. In M. Lewis & J. M. Haviland (Eds.), *Handbook of Emotions*. 2nd ed., (pp. 573–593). New York: Guilford.

Olfson, M. & Marcus, S. C. (2009) National Patterns in Antidepressant Medication Treatment. *Archives of General Psychiatry*, 66(8), 848-856.

Perry. B. (2001) Keep the Cool in School: Self-Regulation – The Second Core Strength. *Early Childhood Today*. Scholastic. Retrieved from: http://www2.scholastic.com.

Raver, C. C. & Knitzer, J. (2002) Ready to Enter: What research tells policymakers about strategies to promote social and emotional school readiness among three- and four-year-old children. New York, NY: National Center for Children in Poverty. Mailman School of Public Health, Columbia University.

Ricard, M. (2007) *Happiness: A Guide to Developing Life's Most Important Skill*. New York: Atlantic Books.

Roth, G., Assor, A., Niemiec, C. P., Ryan, R. M., & Deci, E. L. (2009) The emotional and academic consequences of parental conditional regard: Comparing conditional positive regard, conditional negative regard, and autonomy support as parenting practices. *Developmental Psychology*, 45, 1119–1142.

Szalavitz, M. & Perry, B. D. (2010) *Born for Love: Why Empathy is Essential and Endangered*. New York: Harper Collins.

Shonkoff, J. P. & Phillips, D. A. (Eds.) (2000) *From Neurons to Neighborhoods: The Science of Early Childhood Development*. Washington, DC: National Academy Press.

Spradlin, S. (2003) *Don't Let Your Emotions Run Your Life: How Dialectical Behavior Therapy Can Put You In Control*. Oakland, CA: New Harbinger Publications, Inc.

Strayer, J. & Roberts, W. (2004) Empathy and Observed Anger and Aggression in Five-year Olds. *Social Development*, 13, 1-13.

Vohs, K. D. & Baumeister, R. F. (2011) *Handbook of Self-Regulation: Research, Theory, and Applications*. New York: Guilford Press.

Willoughby, M., Kupersmidt, J. B., & Bryant, D. (2001) Overt and covert dimensions of antisocial behavior in early childhood. *Journal of Abnormal Child Psychology*, 29: 177-187.

Becky A. Bailey, Ph.D., is an award-winning author, renowned teacher and internationally recognized expert in childhood education and developmental psychology.

She is the creator of Conscious Discipline, which is used internationally in public and private schools, child development centers, on military bases and in homes. Over 400,000 copies of her top-selling books are in circulation, including her most recent, *Creating the School Family: Bully-Proofing Classrooms Through Emotional Intelligence*. Parents rave about *Easy to Love, Difficult to Discipline*, a title that has received national acclaim and is published in nine languages. She also touches children's hearts with her award-winning children's book series and six musical CDs.

Dr. Bailey is the founder of Loving Guidance, Inc., dedicated to creating positive environments for children, families and schools. With thirty-five years of experience successfully working with the most difficult children, Dr. Bailey deeply believes we must transform the lives of adults first and children second. She lives in Oviedo, FL. See her on YouTube or visit ConsciousDiscipline.com.